Best wishes
from
Peter Tuffrey

a signed edition from

GREAT NORTHERN

EAST MIDLANDS
STEAM
1950-1966

PETER TUFFREY

GREAT N ORTHERN

ACKNOWLEDGEMENTS

I am grateful for the help received from the following people: Roger Arnold, Ben Brooksbank, David Burrill, John Chalcraft, John Clayson, John Law, Hugh Parkin, Bill Reed, Andrew, Rachel and Sue Warnes, Tony Watson.

Gratitude should also be expressed to my son Tristram for his general help and encouragement throughout the course of the project.

Great Northern Books
PO Box 1380, Bradford, BD5 5FB
www.greatnorthernbooks.co.uk

ISBN: 978-1-914227-05-9

Design and layout: David Burrill

CIP Data
A catalogue for this book is available from the British Library

INTRODUCTION

With an area of just over 6,000 sq. miles, the East Midlands covers a diverse territory, ranging from the Peak District in the north west to Derby and across to the levels of Lincolnshire, then up to the coast at Skegness. In the 1950s and 1960s, the region's railways offered a similarly varied scene that attracted enthusiasts with their cameras to capture the disappearing age of steam.

The East Midlands is formed from several counties: Derbyshire, Leicestershire, Lincolnshire (though not the northernmost part), Northamptonshire, Nottinghamshire and Rutland. In addition to the cities of Derby, Leicester, Lincoln, and Nottingham, there are a number of large towns, such as Chesterfield, Grantham, Kettering, Loughborough, Mansfield, Northampton and Wellingborough, etc.

Like many other areas around the country, the industrial revolution, particularly the exploitation of minerals, encouraged local business people to adopt the canals and wagonways then being introduced to move goods. The East Midlands was particularly rich in coal, as well as ironstone and limestone, which prompted early schemes. For example, the Mansfield & Pinxton Railway connected Mansfield with the Cromford Canal in 1819. Also, the Leicester & Swannington Railway opened in 1832 to transport coal from north west of Leicester to the city and was engineered by early railway pioneer George Stephenson.

A short time later, Stephenson was back in the area to survey a route from Derby northward to Leeds. The aim was to increase the industrial reach of the area, as connections could be made in the north with the Manchester & Leeds Railway, the York & North Midland Railway and south to the Birmingham & Derby Junction Railway and the Midland Counties Railway (Rugby to Leicester, Loughborough, Nottingham and Derby). Construction began in the late 1830s and the line was ready for traffic in 1840. The improved communications (almost Nationwide) led to a boom in business and prosperity for owners and workers alike. With this came the 'Railway Mania' of the early 1840s where a number of railway schemes – both good and bad – were promoted.

Just before this bubble finally burst, several companies had taken a strong position to join forces and were later able to pick and choose future schemes. Several of the above mentioned companies amalgamated to form the Midland Railway in 1844 and this concern went on to dominate much of the East Midlands through to the Grouping of 1923.

The rise of the MR did not proceed unopposed. By the late 1840s, the Great Northern Railway was proceeding with the project of connecting London to the North of England. First joining Peterborough with Spalding, Boston, Lincoln and Doncaster in 1848/1849, the company soon had the line between London and Peterborough ready to allow a competing route between the north and south. This was improved in 1852 with the opening of the Peterborough-Grantham section of the GNR main line.

The competition between the two companies came to a head in 1852 with the opening of Grantham station. A direct service from King's Cross to Nottingham was advertised and worked to Grantham by the GNR, where the Ambergate, Nottingham, Boston & Eastern Junction Railway line was taken. The latter company took the train onward to Nottingham, where the MR's station was shared, using a GNR locomotive. The MR was not pleased with this action and duly corralled the locomotive into a shed and lifted the rail, virtually impounding the engine, which required a lengthy legal process to retrieve. The GNR eventually took over the ANB&ER in the mid-1850s and a new station was built in Nottingham.

The GNR consolidated the company's position in Lincolnshire with an alliance with the Boston, Sleaford & Midland Counties Railway. Worked from the outset by the GNR, the line was taken over completely in the mid-1860s and at this time plans for an extension to Lincoln were put into action. This provided an alternative route between Nottingham and Lincoln, which the MR had monopolised from the 1840s.

The MR's favourable position in the area around Nottingham, Derby and northward along the Erewash Valley to Chesterfield led to bitterness from local businesses, as there was no opportunity to negotiate the set rates. Overtures were made to the GNR for an extension of the ANB&ER line from Nottingham to Derby, Burton-on-Trent and Stafford and plans for this began in the early 1870s. Instead of cutting through Nottingham, the GNR decided to loop round to the north and pass through Ilkeston to reach Derby and beyond. This gave the company opportunity to extend northward and challenge the MR in the Erewash Valley for the coal reserves being exploited there. When this was completed in the later 1870s, the GNR turned to the Leen Valley and laid a line there during the early 1880s; by the turn of the century this had extended to Langwith on the Chesterfield to Lincoln line, opened by the Lancashire, Derbyshire & East Coast Railway and later purchased by the Great Central Railway.

The GNR was not the only company ready to challenge the MR, as the Manchester, Sheffield & Lincolnshire Railway (later Great Central Railway) under Sir Edward Watkin had plans from the 1860s to reach London. Opposition to this proposal did not deter his grand idea and the first section of the eventual GCR main line, or 'London Extension', ran from Woodhouse Junction (on the Sheffield-Lincoln line) to Annesley, opening in the early 1890s; a loop to serve Chesterfield was also built at this time. With parliamentary approval for the remaining 92 miles southward to the capital obtained soon after the Derbyshire Extension, construction began in earnest and was fully completed in April 1899, having cost well over £11,000,000.

With three main railway companies operating in the East Midlands in the early 20th century – also the London & North Western Railway to a lesser extent in the south and south east of the area – passengers and business owners were well-served by the various lines. Yet, this competitive network would ultimately prove unsustainable. This point was highlighted when the railways were Nationalised during the First World War, as Minister of Transport Eric Geddes saw the duplication of lines as wasteful. Whilst opposed to full government control, Geddes preferred locally managed companies to oversee the lines in an efficient way. The result of this was the Grouping of 1923 and the MR became a constituent of the London, Midland & Scottish Railway, whilst the GNR and GCR became part of the London & North Eastern Railway.

The Grouping perhaps did little to alter the operations of lines in the East Midlands as industrial output continued to require transportation on the various routes, in addition to passengers travelling freely between locations. Not until after the Second World War and the formation of British Railways under the government did real change occur. This was mainly due to policy and the change in times. BR decided to pursue dieselisation of the locomotive fleet in the mid-1950s and rationalisation of running lines due to falling usage. The rise of private car ownership and the government's promotion of road haulage of goods was the cause of falling passenger and freight receipts. The latter revenue had always underpinned the railways and the loss could not be replaced.

The 'Beeching Axe' was a futile attempt at making BR more profitable by closing duplicated routes and those with low passenger numbers. The East Midlands was hit by several closures, including the whole GCR main line and much of the GNR network. Also, the MR line from Mansfield to Newark, which saw Mansfield station closed completely, leaving the town with the dubious honour of being one of the largest in Britain without a station for a number of years. Beeching closures were not popular with many at the time and subsequently attempts have been made to reopen some routes. This occurred in the early 1990s with the Nottingham-Worksop, or 'Robin Hood', line which uses part of the old MR and GNR routes in the area.

Locomotives at work in the East Midlands were diverse. Ex-MR engines continued to be seen into the mid-1960s, including Johnson 0-6-0s and 0-6-0Ts which were in use from the latter half of the 19th century. Much of the motive power on ex-MR lines was from the LMSR standard classes, such as Fowler 4F 0-6-0s, Stanier 8F Class 2-8-0s, Class 5 4-6-0s and 'Jubilee' Class 4-6-0s, as well as Fairburn 4P Class 2-6-4Ts and Ivatt 2-6-0s and 2-6-2Ts.

For the old GNR routes, many of Sir Nigel Gresley's designs were in evidence, such as K2 and K3 2-6-0s, J39 Class 0-6-0s and O2 Class 2-8-0s for freight, A3 Class and A4 Pacifics for expresses on the East Coast Main Line and V2 Class 2-6-2s on both passenger and freight. The later LNER designs of Edward Thompson and A.H. Peppercorn also worked hard in the East Midlands, with Thompson O1 2-8-0s used on the ex-GCR main line 'Windcutter' freight trains, his B1 4-6-0s on many passenger and goods services and the L1 2-6-4T had a role hauling local passenger trains. Peppercorn A1 Pacifics were on the main line with principal expresses and the K1 2-6-0 was normally on freight duties, though could be pressed on to passenger trains. GCR types from J.G. Robinson mixed together with the aforementioned LNER designs, particularly the O4 (GCR 8K) Class 2-8-0s, both in original form and rebuilt by both Gresley and Thompson, on coal trains, whilst the A5 4-6-2T was regularly on local trains, as were the D11 Class 4-4-0s, though these travelled slightly further.

British Railways chose to continue with steam immediately after Nationalisation and introduced a number of standard classes to replace older types and improve services. One of the most visible was the 9F 2-10-0, which quickly mastered coal and iron ore trains alike, and the ten Franco-Crosti boiler variants were housed at Wellingborough. Class 5 and Class 4 4-6-0s appeared in the area on passenger services, whilst Class 2 2-6-0s and 2-6-2Ts handled the locals. Later, BR Standard Class 7 Pacifics worked on cross-country freight and passenger trains.

Used in a supporting role, though no less important, was the small army of industrial locomotives employed at collieries and quarries. As mentioned, the coalfields of Nottingham and Derby were heavily exploited and shunting of loaded and empty wagons on site was performed by 0-4-0ST and 0-6-0ST engines of varying vintages. The same was true for the iron ore and limestone which was exploited in the Kettering/Corby area and in the Peak District respectively. Power stations, such as Castle Donington, and Chemical Works – of the Staveley Company – also had locomotives, with the latter having an arrangement to lease from the MR, LMSR and BR.

East Midlands Steam, 1950-1966, captures the twilight years of steam traction in the area through evocative colour and black-and-white images. Many of these have been taken at the area's principal stations, sheds and industrial locations, as well as smaller stations and from lineside. The 'glory days' of steam are now in excess of 50 years in the past, yet for many they are still more than worth remembering. Hopefully, this collection keeps those memories alive now and in the future.

Peter Tuffrey
Doncaster, February 2021

Above ALFRETON & SOUTH NORMANTON STATION

A southbound train of empty coal wagons travels along the slow line at Alfreton & South Normanton station on 23rd June 1961. Leading is 4F Class 0-6-0 no. 43850. Photograph by B.W.L. Brooksbank.

Below ANNESLEY SHED

Several Thompson O1 Class 2-8-0s are in the yard at Annesley shed on 18th August 1962, with no. 63789 the focus of attention. Rebuilt from Robinson O4 specifications in January 1946, the locomotive was allocated to Annesley four years later and ultimately condemned there in November 1962. Photograph by Paul Tusan courtesy Rail Photoprints.

ASLOCKTON

A local train from Nottingham to Grantham – hauled by Gresley J39 Class 0-6-0 no. 64955 – pauses at Aslockton station in the 1950s. The station opened with the line in 1850, yet the main building (right) was not added until 1857. Designed by local architect Thomas Chambers Hine, the structure has since been demolished, though the stop remains active.

Photograph courtesy Rail-Online.

Above BAGTHORPE JUNCTION

Thompson B1 Class 4-6-0 no. 61250 *A. Harold Bibby* travels northward with an express near Bagthorpe Junction, Basford, Nottingham, on 7th August 1960. The first bridge in the background carried the ex-Great Central main line over the ex-Great Northern Railway's Derbyshire Extension line, with the junction being made between the two a little to the south. Photograph by Bill Reed.

Below BAGTHORPE JUNCTION

Colwick-allocated Gresley J39 Class 0-6-0 no. 64827 has a local service northbound at Bagthorpe Junction on 20th September 1958. The engine had been there from 1947 and in 1959 moved on to Doncaster where withdrawal occurred in February 1960. Photograph by Bill Reed.

Above **BASFORD NORTH STATION**

The Midland Railway dominated the area around Nottingham and Derby during the mid-19th century. When the Great Northern Railway proposed a new line from the east of Nottingham to Derby and Burton-on-Trent, also connecting with existing lines to Stafford, the scheme received support as a much-needed competitor to the MR. Construction for the route began in the early 1870s and opened in sections to 1878. Basford North station was opened on the line on 1st February 1876 as New Basford, then six months later the title was changed to Basford & Bulwell. On 21st September 1953 a further change to Basford North occurred and this title was used until closure on 7th September 1964. Thompson B1 no. 61209 is just leaving the station with the 13.22 service to Nottingham via Gedling in March 1958. The line to the left of the locomotive is the connection to the ex-GCR line and the over bridge is the one visible in the images on page seven and bottom of page nine. Photograph by Bill Reed.

Opposite above **BASFORD**

View eastward to Arnold Road, Basford, on 25th April 1960. Gresley K3 Class 2-6-0 no. 61896 is approaching Basford North station with a semi-fitted freight from Colwick to Burton-on-Trent. The locomotive was one of ninety-three classmembers built by Darlington Works, entering traffic in August 1930. No. 61896 had transferred from Gorton, Manchester, to Colwick shed in June 1954 and was condemned at the latter during May 1962. Photograph by Bill Reed.

Opposite below **BAGTHORPE JUNCTION**

BR Standard Class 5 4-6-0 no. 73158 was one of the final batch of seventeen locomotives constructed, being completed at Doncaster Works in December 1956. The engine was also one of five from this order allocated to Neasden for employment on the Marylebone to Sheffield expresses. Yet, these locomotives were considered underpowered for the duty, which was previously undertaken by Gresley A3 Pacifics and V2 Class 2-6-2s, and no. 73158 was one of three Class 5s swapped with King's Cross in late 1957. Working there for a year, the locomotive had spells at Sheffield Darnall, Neasden, Derby and Neasden again to June 1962 when the last mentioned closed, resulting in a transfer to Cricklewood. Working from the latter when pictured here at Bagthorpe Junction on 2nd March 1963, no. 73158 was transferred to Patricroft a year later and withdrawn there in October 1967. Photograph by Bill Reed.

Above BINGHAM STATION

Designed for the suburban traffic of the Great Central Railway running in and out of Marylebone station, J.G. Robinson's 9N Class (LNER A5) 4-6-2T was master of this task for well over 30 years. Introduced in 1911 as one of the earliest from the company to feature a superheater in the boiler, 21 were erected at Gorton before Grouping, whilst a further 10 appeared just after; Gresley later ordered 13 from Hawthorn, Leslie & Co. for work in the North East. Most of the class were based at Neasden shed until after Nationalisation when new classes spurred the process of dispersal to other parts of the system. No. 69804, which was an early example, constructed in May 1911, transferred from Neasden to Lincoln in 1950. Over a few months in 1955 several moves occurred to Immingham, Boston and Langwith Junction before the locomotive settled at Colwick for the final three years in service. Whilst in Lincolnshire and Nottinghamshire, the engine was employed on local passenger services and has one here at Bingham station – between Nottingham and Grantham – in the second half of the 1950s. Photograph courtesy Rail-Online.

Opposite above BLISWORTH

The London & Birmingham Railway passed through the countryside just to the north of the village of Blisworth and a small station was provided on opening in 1838. Lying between Northampton and Towcester, the station later provided an important junction for lines to the two places, as well as the main line promoting the exploitation of limestone and iron ore in the area. This led to the expansion of the station and associated facilities later in the 19th century, with extensive sidings established for the assembly of iron ore trains. Here, under the gantries for the West Coast Main Line electrification scheme, BR Standard Class 9F no. 92230 moves off with a load of iron ore on 28th September 1964. Photograph by Revd J. David Benson courtesy A1 Steam Trust.

Opposite below BLISWORTH

The West Coast Main Line was electrified in stages as part of British Railways' Modernisation Plan of 1955. Starting with Crewe to Manchester in 1960, Crewe to Liverpool followed in 1962, then focussing on the southern half to London which was completed in 1965. Stanier 8F no. 48688 is under the wires at Blisworth on 28th September 1964, heading a northbound limestone train. The locomotive was Bletchley allocated at this time and was withdrawn shortly after a move to Northampton in July 1965. Photograph by Revd J. David Benson courtesy A1 Steam Trust.

Above **BOSTON STATION**

Thompson B1 Class 4-6-0 no. 61188 passes through Boston station with the 12.05 service from Mablethorpe to Nottingham Victoria on 25th July 1964. The engine had a long-standing association with ex-GCR lines, being based at Gorton, Leicester and Colwick over a career that spanned just over 18 years, 1947-1965. Photograph by B.W.L. Brooksbank.

Below **BOSTON SHED**

On 18th March 1956, Gresley J39 Class 0-6-0 no. 64712 is serviced at Boston shed. The engine was Lincoln-based, though a brief allocation to Boston occurred between November 1958 and March 1959. Photograph courtesy Rail-Online.

Above BULWELL COMMON STATION

Opened by the Great Central Railway in March 1899, Bulwell Common station had recently closed when pictured here on 12th July 1963. On a single island platform in the midst of the running lines, the station was later cleared and a housing development has claimed the land. In the foreground is a 20-ton express goods brake van, built at Faverdale in 1940 to diagram 158. Photograph by B.W.L. Brooksbank.

Below BULWELL COMMON

The GNR built a second line northward after reaching Derby in the 1870s. This departed from the main route north of Bagthorpe Junction and reached several collieries through to Kirkby-in-Ashfield and beyond. Stanier 8F no. 48699 is just north of Bulwell Common station here, taking the curve to Moorbridge Junction with a train of empties on 27th August 1966. Photograph by Bill Reed.

Above BULWELL MARKET STATION

Luckily for these young 'spotters', the number of this locomotive has been cleaned off, allowing another engine to be recorded in their notebooks. Fairburn 4P Class 2-6-4T no. 42218 is the locomotive in question and has a local service to Worksop at Bulwell Market station on 10th October 1964. The station was one of several in the area as the GCR, GNR and Midland Railway all had lines running through. Bulwell Market was in fact the first when opened by the latter company in 1848 on completion of the line from Nottingham to Mansfield. Originally known as just Bulwell, 'Market' was added in 1952 and in use until closure 12 years later. Resurrected in the mid-1990s, the station also boasts a tram stop following the completion of the system in 2004. Photograph by Geoff Warnes.

Opposite above BULWELL MARKET STATION

View south from Highbury Road to Bulwell Market station on 21st August 1963. Photograph by B.W.L. Brooksbank.

Opposite below BUXTON STATION

Hughes 'Crab' Class 2-6-0 no. 42943 is at Buxton station on 18th May 1960. Allocated to the town's depot from April 1939, the locomotive was soon to move on, taking a berth at Stockport at the end of the year. Photograph by Geoff Warnes.

Above BUXTON SHED

The London & North Western Railway and Midland Railway companies both promoted schemes for lines reaching Buxton from the north and south respectively. The LNWR established servicing facilities near the station when the line became operational in 1863 and this was active until the end of the 19th century. A new depot was constructed at this time further north on the eastern side of the line from Stockport and had six lines under cover, with associated facilities provided. The shed managed to survive until quite late, being closed in March 1968. Stanier 8F Class 2-8-0 no. 48165 is one of several engines 'on shed' during a visit on 11th May 1963. This was part of the 'North Midlands Railtour' organised by the Railway Correspondence & Travel Society and Locomotive Club of Great Britain, running from London St Pancras to Buxton. No. 48165, which has a Fowler tender, had two spells at Buxton, 1955-1958 and 1960-1964. Photograph by B.W.L. Brooksbank.

Opposite above CADLEY HILL COLLIERY, SWADLINCOTE

Located just a few miles south east of Burton-on-Trent, Cadley Hill Colliery was sunk in 1860 and operational until 1988 when the last working mine in the area. W.G. Bagnall 0-6-0ST locomotive, works no. 3059, *Florence No. 2* is shunting wagons at the colliery during the mid-1970s. The locomotive had started life in 1954 and sent to work at Florence Colliery, Trentham, south of Stoke-on-Trent. Following the introduction of diesels there at the end of the 1960s, *Florence No. 2* managed to survive until 1975 when dispatched to Cadley Hill. After three years the engine was allowed to retire to the Battlefield Line Railway, later moving to the Foxfield Railway. Operational there for a time, *Florence No. 2* is currently awaiting restoration. Photograph by John Law.

Opposite below CADLEY HILL COLLIERY, SWADLINCOTE

Another W.G. Bagnall 0-6-0ST locomotive employed at Cadley Hill Colliery was *Empress* (works no. 3061), also built in 1954. Previously, the engine had been employed at Measham Colliery, Leicestershire, arriving at Cadley Hill in July 1970. At this time *Empress* was named, earlier being known as No. 6. In 1987 the locomotive was preserved, running on the Mangapps Farm Railway. Following a restoration in the early 2010s, *Empress* was transferred to a new home at the Pontypool & Blaenavon Railway. Photograph by Bill Reed.

Above CHESTERFIELD MARKET PLACE STATION

The Lancashire, Derbyshire & East Coast Railway was promoted to connect the North West with the Lincolnshire coast, yet in the event only a small portion of the envisaged route was constructed. This was between Chesterfield and Lincoln and opened for passenger traffic in 1897. The terminus at Chesterfield was located south west of the Market Place and this title was later adopted in 1907 following the takeover of the company by the Great Central Railway, which already had a station in use. With three stations at Chesterfield, BR saw fit to close Market Place station in 1951 and the remains are seen here, c. 1960; the area was redeveloped in the early 1970s. Photograph by Geoff Warnes.

Opposite above CADLEY HILL COLLIERY, SWADLINCOTE

The coal stock of *Cadley Hill No. 1* looks to be in the process of being replenished at the colliery in June 1974. This locomotive was not the first to carry the name, however, as an Andrew Barclay 0-6-0ST, works no. 2185, had the honour for eight years before scrapped in late 1970. The name was transferred to Hunslet Engine Co. 0-6-0ST, works no. 3851, shortly after the locomotive arrived from Nailstone Coal Preparation Plant (where the engine had been delivered new in 1962) around the same time as the predecessor's demise. *Cadley Hill No. 1* continued in service at the colliery until 1985 when transferred to Snibston. A year later, the locomotive was taken on by Leicester Museums as the colliery site was transformed into Snibston Discovery Park. This endeavour lasted until 2015 when the museum was demolished and the land sold for housing, whilst the locomotive was placed in storage. Photograph by Bill Reed.

Opposite below CASTLE DONINGTON POWER STATION

Built in 1958, Castle Donington Power Station received two new 0-4-0ST locomotives to shunt coal wagons around the site. These were built by Robert Stephenson & Hawthorns and numbered 1 and 2, with works nos 7817 and 7818 respectively. Central Electricity Generating Board (CEGB) 1 is at work on site in August 1971. Both engines saw the demise of the power station in the mid-1990s and the pair went into preservation, with no. 1 eventually settling at the Midland Railway, Butterley, where the engine awaits an overhaul at the time of writing. Photograph by Bill Reed.

Above CHEE DALE

'Royal Scot' Class 4-6-0 no. 46122 *Royal Ulster Rifleman* has a southbound express on the 1 in 101 climb to Peak Forest and is approaching Chee Tor tunnels at Chee Dale in 1959. The locomotive has '9E' on the shed plate, denoting an allocation to Trafford Park shed which lasted from April to June of that year. Photograph courtesy Rail Photoprints.

Opposite above CHESTERFIELD

A southbound freight train approaches Chesterfield Midland station on 14th March 1959. The locomotive is BR Standard Class 9F 2-10-0 no. 92024 which is equipped with a Franco-Crosti boiler. This saw exhaust gasses and steam diverted through a secondary chamber to heat water before entering the boiler in an effort to improve efficiency; several systems to achieve this had been tested on steam locomotives previously. The Franco-Crosti boiler ultimately failed to provide distinct advantages and the ten Standard Class 9Fs fitted were subsequently equipped with normal boilers. No. 92024, which was built at Crewe Works in June 1955, was transformed in February 1960 and continued in service until November 1967. From new until 1964, the engine was allocated to Wellingborough shed. Photograph by B.W.L. Brooksbank.

Opposite Below CHESTERFIELD

A stray locomotive has been captured at Chesterfield on 13th June 1957 as Thompson B1 Class 4-6-0 no. 61239 of Carlisle Canal shed has an unidentified special travelling northward. The engine was new to York depot in 1947 and was there for six years before moving to Carlisle. This allocation lasted until June 1962 and two months were spent at Gorton before withdrawal. Photograph by B.W.L. Brooksbank.

Above CHINLEY STATION

Stanier 'Jubilee' Class 4-6-0 no. 45648 *Wemyss* has an express from Manchester to Derby at Chinley station during August 1960. The station was opened in 1867 as the Midland Railway extended the already existing line between Ambergate, north of Derby, and Rowsley towards Stockport and Manchester. The MR later built a line from Dore, south west of Sheffield, in 1894 and Chinley became a busy junction between the two lines, resulting in the construction of a new station in 1902. This survives today, though only the line from Sheffield continues to carry traffic. Photograph by Alan H. Bryant courtesy Rail Photoprints.

Opposite above CHESTERFIELD

A short distance to the north of Chesterfield Midland station, three trains pass each other on 24th March 1953. Stanier 8F Class 2-8-0 no. 48095 is travelling southward on the up fast line with empty mineral wagons, whilst classmate no. 48461 is on the down goods line with an iron ore train. On the far right with a permanent way train is Johnson 3F Class 0-6-0 no. 43254. Photograph by B.W.L. Brooksbank.

Opposite below CHESTERFIELD

The Somerset & Dorset Joint Railway was an undertaking that linked the Midlands with the South Coast. Initially an independent company, the venture failed and was taken over by the Midland Railway and London & South Western Railway. The aforementioned company was responsible for the locomotive stock employed and used their own designs. In the mid-1890s, five 0-6-0s were built at Derby Works to the 1798 Class then being built in numbers for the MR and dispatched for use by the S&DJR. As no. 66, this locomotive, no. 43211, worked on the line until the late 1940s when taken into stock by the London, Midland & Scottish Railway. At Nationalisation, no. 43211 was allocated to Hasland shed (south of Chesterfield) and this was the case until December 1958 when moved on to Trafford Park. The locomotive was ultimately withdrawn from there in July 1961. No. 43211 is at Chesterfield Midland station on 5th September 1957 just departing with a goods train. Photograph courtesy Rail-Online.

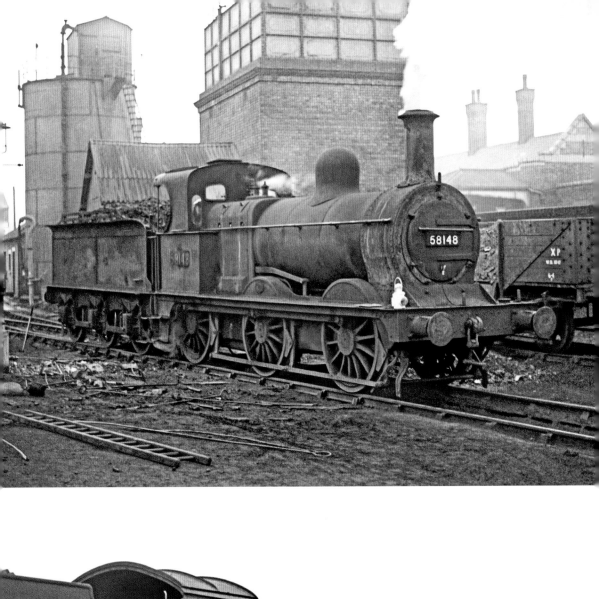

Above COLWICK SHED

Just east of Nottingham city centre, Colwick shed was established when the GNR expanded the company's presence in the area during the 1870s. The depot mainly served the coal traffic, which was extensive, and this soon found facilities inadequate. Extensions were necessary in the early 1880s and again before the turn of the century when around 100 engines were housed, with facilities for repairs. Major improvements were made in the late 1930s, with the 500-ton mechanical coaler (in the background here) installed. Gresley K2 Class 2-6-0 no. 61753 is in the yard during the late 1950s; withdrawal from Colwick occurred in September 1959. Photograph by Bill Reed.

Opposite above COALVILLE SHED

Johnson 1142 (2F) Class 0-6-0 no. 58148 was amongst the few surviving class members when pictured at Coalville shed on 14th December 1963. The locomotive was constructed by Beyer Peacock in March 1876 and survived until the end of 1963, with no. 58182 the last of the design condemned early in 1964. No. 58148 began life as no. 1199, later becoming no. 2967 in 1907, then having 20,000 added in 1934. The engine had several modifications over the 87 years in traffic, including the increase of cylinder diameter from 17½ to 18 in. diameter by 26 in. stroke, a G6 boiler with Belpaire firebox replaced the original type with round-top firebox and a new set of frames was also provided. Photograph by Neville Simms from the Ranwell Collection courtesy Rail Photoprints.

Opposite below COLWICK SHED

J.G. Robinson designed the 8K Class 2-8-0 for the GCR's heavy freight traffic in 1911. In just a short time, 126 locomotives were erected by the company's Gorton Works, Kitson & Co. and the North British Locomotive Company. No. 63707 was one of these GCR engines and amongst 20 built by Kitson & Co., entering traffic in August 1912. During the First World War, the 8K design was deemed suitable for use by the Railway Operating Division and just over 500 were constructed. Nearly 300 were later bought by the London & North Eastern Railway, joining the GCR engines in forming Class O4. No. 63707 is at Colwick shed on 11th January 1964. The engine was employed there from September 1962 until condemned in July 1965. Photograph by Neville Simms from the Ranwell Collection courtesy Rail Photoprints.

Above CORBY PEN GREEN SHED

Several of the locomotives (nos 56, 63, 57 and 62 identified) employed at the steel works at Corby have a break outside Pen Green shed on 14th September 1965. Photograph by Hugh Ballantyne courtesy Rail Photoprints.

Below CORBY STEELWORKS

No. 18 has a short train of hopper wagons on the weighbridge at Corby steelworks during March 1970. Built by Robert Stephenson & Co. in 1936, the locomotive was delivered new to the steelworks (then owned by Stewarts & Lloyds) and worked there until scrapped in late 1972. Photograph courtesy Rail Photoprints.

Above COLWICK SHED

Holden J69 Class 0-6-0T no. 68522 was allocated to Colwick shed from August 1958 to November 1959 when transferred to Boston. Photograph by Bill Reed.

Below COLWICK SHED

Robinson O4 Class 2-8-0 no. 63873 was built for the ROD in May 1919, though did not enter service for the LNER until 1927. The engine, which was a long-term resident at Colwick, has been fitted with a B1-type boiler and cab, resulting in an O4/8 sub-classification. Photograph by Bill Reed.

Above DERBY MIDLAND STATION

Long-term Leeds Holbeck shed resident, Stanier 'Jubilee' 4-6-0 no. 45675 *Hardy* approaches Derby Midland station on 8th February 1964. The locomotive has a Leeds to Bristol service. Photograph by Neville Simms from the Ranwell Collection courtesy Rail Photoprints.

Below DERBY ST ANDREWS SIDINGS

The London & North Western Railway established a goods station, named St Andrews at Grouping, to the south of the station in the mid-19th century. Fowler 4P Compound 4-4-0 no. 41102 appears to be out of service in the station sidings in the late 1950s. Photograph by Bill Reed.

Above DERBY MIDLAND STATION

View eastward towards Derby Works from Derby station on 4th April 1965, with Stanier Class 5 no. 44861 seen on a permanent way train. The engine was approaching the end of a six-month spell at Derby shed, moving on to Newton Heath, where withdrawal occurred in November 1967. Photograph by Geoff Warnes.

Below CORBY

Robert Stephenson & Hawthorns 0-6-0ST no. 62 is at work on an iron ore train at the Corby quarry in August 1968. Arriving new at the site in 1950, during 1969 the locomotive was preserved at the Keighley & Worth Valley Railway, later moving several times and is currently at the Spa Valley Railway. Photograph courtesy Rail Photoprints.

Above DERBY MIDLAND STATION
Ex-works Fowler 3F 0-6-0T no. 47476 has been tasked with turning this train of Royal Mail carriages via the Chaddesden Loop on 14th June 1957. The engine was regularly employed at Holyhead shed and was condemned there in 1964. Photograph by B.W.L. Brooksbank.

Below DERBY MIDLAND STATION
A pair of withdrawn locomotives is pictured from Derby Midland station, likely arriving for scrapping at the works on 13th April 1960. On the left is Fowler 7F Class 2-8-0 no. 53802 (from Bath Green Park) and right Fowler 3F Class 43664 (Canklow). Photograph by B.W.L. Brooksbank.

Above DERBY MIDLAND STATION

View south from Derby Midland station as Johnson 3F Class 0-6-0 no. 43657 travels tender first with a train of coal wagons. Built by Vulcan Foundry during 1900, the locomotive had just been refreshed at Derby Works and is being 'run in' before returning northward to Warrington Dallam depot. The engine was a long-term resident there, being withdrawn at the shed in October 1962. Photograph by B.W.L. Brooksbank.

Below DERBY MIDLAND STATION

Travelling northward away from Derby Midland station on 24th June 1964 is Fowler 4F Class 0-6-0 no. 44118. Even though pictured in the height of summer, the locomotive betrays evidence of tasks undertaken in the winter months. The main feature is the roll-off cover and boxed-in sides of the coal space in the tender, also a large hole in the side of the bufferbeam. All were features to make the engine suitable for clearing snow drifts. Photograph by B.W.L. Brooksbank.

Above DERBY MIDLAND STATION

Fowler 4F Class 0-6-0 no. 44454 has a train of coal empties passing Derby Midland station around 1962/1963. The locomotive was erected at Crewe Works in February 1928 and had a service life of 35 years, being withdrawn in October 1963 from Derby. Photograph courtesy Rail Photoprints.

Opposite above DERBY

View north east from London Road, Derby, to number four shed and the works, with Stanier 'Jubilee' Class no. 45585 *Hyderabad* in the foreground on the turntable near the old North Staffordshire Railway engine shed site. The latter building had been erected in the early 1870s and was in use until after Grouping when demolished. Number four shed was opened in 1890 and used until 1967; the building comprised two roundhouses. No. 45585, which is pictured in September 1963, had arrived at Derby shed in January and was condemned there in May 1964. The engine had several spells at the depot previously: 1937-1940; 1944; 1947-1952; 1953-1957. Photograph courtesy Rail Photoprints.

Opposite below DERBY MIDLAND STATION

On 14th October 1962, Fowler 'Patriot' Class 4-6-0 no. 45543 *Home Guard* reverses towards Derby Midland station in order to take on the Locomotive Club of Great Britain's 'Midland Limited' railtour. This had begun the day at London Marylebone station behind Raven B16 Class 4-6-0 no. 61438 and travelled to Nottingham Victoria where Robinson J11 Class 0-6-0 no. 64354 had taken over for the short journey to Burton-on-Trent. Johnson 3F 0-6-0 no. 43658 deposited the party at Derby station, travelling from Burton via Long Eaton. From Derby, no. 45543 worked as far as Northampton, handing the reins to Stanier Class 5 no. 45392 for the run back to London, though terminating at St Pancras. No. 45543 was the last un-rebuilt 'Patriot' Class locomotive still at work and just a month later the engine was sent for scrap. Photograph by Bill Reed.

Above DERBY SHED

In the early 1930s, the London, Midland & Scottish Railway ordered five shunting locomotives from Kitson & Co., Leeds. These were later augmented by five further engines built at Horwich Works under British Railways in 1953/1954, with no. 47006 amongst this batch and completed during November 1953. Delivered new to Birkenhead, no. 47006 was much-travelled, having allocations to Bangor, Chester, Widnes, Derby, Hasland, Burton, Coalville and Rowsley. The locomotive had several spells at Derby, being photographed here during April 1963, which was part of the penultimate posting – September 1962 to November 1963. Withdrawal occurred in August 1966. Photograph courtesy Rail Photoprints.

Opposite DERBY SHED

Stanier 4P Class 2-6-4T no. 42636 had a mishap at Derby shed on 24th April 1963, falling into the 70ft turntable pit outside the depot. The accident proved fatal for the locomotive as withdrawal was seen more economical than repair and the decision was made official in early May. No. 42636 was Nottingham-allocated at the time and had been there from January 1959. Photograph courtesy Rail Photoprints.

Above DERBY ST ANDREWS SIDINGS

Locomotive engineers constantly attempted to make the steam circuit more efficient, therefore saving money on fuel, water, etc. One of the methods employed was compounding, whereby the steam entered a high pressure cylinder and then moved on to a lower pressure cylinder before exhausted into the atmosphere. S.W. Johnson experimented with compounding in the early 20th century for the MR, producing 45 '1000' Class 4-4-0s. Fowler developed the design under the LMSR and 195 4P Class 4-4-0s were erected between 1924 and 1932. Both classes had three cylinders, with the inside high pressure (19 in. diameter by 26 in. stroke) and the outer pair low pressure (21 in. by 26 in.), whilst the 4Ps had a slightly lower working boiler pressure of 200 lb per sq. in. No. 41090 was constructed at Derby Works in July 1925 and in service until December 1958, being one of 36 classmembers condemned in the year. The engine was Derby-allocated from June 1958 and is seen, likely after withdrawal, at St Andrews goods station sidings. Attention appears to have been given to the middle cylinder as the removable footplate piece below the smokebox is now tied to the side of the boiler. Photograph by Bill Reed.

Opposite above DERBY MIDLAND STATION

Though principally dedicated to freight traffic, the BR Standard 9F 2-10-0 was no stranger to passenger services. Initially, this was owing to failures on the road and an unemployed 9F was the best substitute to be found at the time. This likely spurred the authorities into making use of classmembers at peak periods, usually for summer holiday traffic and this was the case from the late 1950s until the end of steam. No. 92139 of Saltley shed, Birmingham, is backing on to a passenger service here at Derby Midland station during summer 1963. Photograph courtesy Rail Photoprints.

Opposite below DESFORD JUNCTION

BR Standard Class 9F no. 92103 travels at speed through Desford Junction, west of Leicester, with a northbound train of mineral wagons on 22nd December 1963. The junction was located just east of Desford station and was the point where the original Leicester & Swannington Railway (opened 1832) diverged to Leicester West Bridge station from the Midland Railway-constructed line from Knighton Junction on the main line. This was part of a larger scheme to connect with Burton-on-Trent and the Leicester & Swannington Railway was purchased and extended for this purpose. Photograph by John Briggs courtesy A1 Steam Trust.

Above EDWINSTOWE STATION

Thompson B1 Class 4-6-0 no. 61209 calls at Edwinstowe station with a local service during the early 1950s. The station was on the Lancashire, Derbyshire & East Coast Railway line from Chesterfield to Lincoln and was open from 1896 to 1956. Photograph courtesy Rail-Online.

Below ESSENDINE STATION

Two locomotives taking on water at Essendine station in 1958 are an unidentified Parker 9F (LNER N5) Class 0-6-2T and Gresley A4 Class Pacific no. 60025 *Falcon*. The station only remained open until mid-1959. Photograph courtesy Rail Photoprints.

Above FARNSFIELD STATION

A special service headed by Fowler 4F no. 44415 is at Farnsfield station on 23rd April 1956. The station was located on the Mansfield to Newark line, though closed to passengers in August 1929. A goods service remained until 1964. Photograph courtesy Rail-Online.

Below FIRSBY STATION

Located on the Grimsby to Boston line, Firsby station was an important exchange point for traffic to Skegness and Spilsby. Gresley K2 Class no. 61755 has a local service to Skegness at the southern end of the loop platform on 30th August 1949. Photograph by T.G. Hepburn from Rail Archive Stephenson courtesy Rail-Online.

Above FOREST TOWN

Just north east of Mansfield at Forest Town, Gresley O2 Class 2-8-0 no. 63977 travels towards Mansfield with three other locomotives during late 1963. The engines are on the Mansfield Railway line which was opened in 1916, mainly as a colliery link between Kirkby-in-Ashfield and the Chesterfield-Lincoln line, joining the latter between Clipstone and Edwinstowe. No. 63977 was withdrawn soon after being pictured here. Photograph by Dave Swale courtesy Rail Photoprints.

Opposite above GAINSBOROUGH CENTRAL STATION

A stopping service is at Gainsborough Central station behind Thompson B1 Class 4-6-0 no. 61212 in the 1950s. From entering traffic in July 1947 until withdrawn in November 1964, the engine was allocated to Retford (GCR) shed. Photograph courtesy Rail-Online.

Opposite below GAINSBOROUGH

A diversion has taken the 'Harrogate Sunday Pullman' off the East Coast Main Line and sent the train via Gainsborough, c. 1960. The service is hauled by Peppercorn A1 Class Pacific no. 60117 *Bois Roussel* of Leeds Copley Hill shed. Photograph courtesy Rail Photoprints.

Opposite above GEDLING

Robinson O4 Class no. 63674 passes the remains of Gedling & Carlton Railway station in the early 1960s. Closed in April 1960, the station had been opened by the Ambergate, Nottingham, Boston & Eastern Junction Railway, later being taken over by the GNR. Photograph by Bill Reed.

Opposite below GEDLING COLLIERY

Peckett & Sons Ltd 0-6-0ST *Catherine* is at Gedling Colliery in the early 1960s. Dating from 1902, the locomotive was working at Gedling when the colliery was Nationalised. *Catherine* was later scrapped on site in the mid-1960s. Photograph by Bill Reed.

Below GEDLING COLLIERY

Built by the Hunslet Engine Co. in 1942, 0-6-0ST *King George* is at Gedling Colliery, east of Nottingham. The locomotive spent much of the 1940s and 1950s at Linby Colliery, with a spell at Bestwood Colliery in the late 1950s, before arriving at Gedling in February 1961. *King George* served on site until 1977 and was subsequently preserved, presently waiting for an overhaul at Didcot Railway Centre. Photograph by Bill Reed.

GLENFIELD STATION
Johnson '1142' Class 0-6-0 no. 58148 is at Glenfield station with a local freight service on 20th October 1962. Photograph by John Briggs courtesy A1 Steam Trust.

Above GLENFIELD STATION

The Leicester West Bridge-Desford Junction section of the Leicester & Swannington Railway was freight-only from the late 1920s to 1966. Ex-MR Johnson 0-6-0s were latterly retained specifically for the freight services on the line. No. 58247 was one and has a train stopped at Glenfield in April 1957. Photograph courtesy Rail Photoprints.

Below GLENFIELD STATION

No. 58148 is about to depart from Glenfield station after shunting wagons on 24th March 1962. The locomotive was condemned at Coalville in December 1963. Photograph by John Briggs courtesy A1 Steam Trust.

GRANTHAM STATION
Peppercorn A1 Class Pacific no. 60120 *Kittiwake* approaches Grantham station with a northbound express in 1962. Photograph by Cedric Clayson courtesy John Clayson.

Above GRANTHAM STATION

Gresley A3 Class Pacific no. 60107 *Royal Lancer* is at Grantham station on 1st June 1963. A King's Cross engine for the last three years, a transfer to Grantham was to occur soon following the closure of King's Cross depot to steam. Photograph by Geoff Warnes.

Below GRANTHAM STATION

Shunting carriages at Grantham is Gresley N2 Class no. 69560. The engine was briefly allocated to Grantham and was resident at the shed from June 1959 to October 1960 when withdrawn. Photograph by Bill Reed.

Above GRANTHAM STATION

The Ambergate, Nottingham, Boston & Eastern Junction Railway constructed the first station in Grantham during 1850 and this was located on a site to the north west of the town. The Great Northern Railway arrived in 1852, with the completion of the line from Peterborough to Retford, and a new station was designed by Henry Goddard, who had a practice in Lincoln and produced the other stations on the section. Construction was carried out by Kirk & Parry of Sleaford. The station was later modified by the LNER in the late 1930s, as work took place to improve the platforms and canopies. Thompson B1 Class 4-6-0 no. 61281 has a train of iron ore empties for High Dyke sidings at Grantham station on 27th January 1962. Photograph by Neville Simms from the Ranwell Collection courtesy Rail Photoprints.

Opposite above GRANTHAM SHED

The GNR established stabling facilities for company locomotives shortly after the opening of the station, building a two-track shed on the west side. This was later extended by two lines and further modifications were made by the end of the century. A new shed was built in addition to the original in 1897, which also had four tracks, as well as a coal stage being erected. The latter is just visible here, though dominated by the Henry Lees & Co. mechanical coaler installed by the LNER. Gresley A3 Pacific no. 60048 *Doncaster* is between duties at the depot in the early 1960s. Photograph by Bill Reed.

Opposite below GRANTHAM STATION

Gresley N2 Class 0-6-2T no. 69505 was erected by the North British Locomotive Company in December 1920 as GNR no. 1726. Hornsey-allocated for much of the BR period, a transfer to Grantham happened in June 1959. The locomotive is seen there around this time shunting a brake van; withdrawal occurred in November 1960. Photograph by Bill Reed.

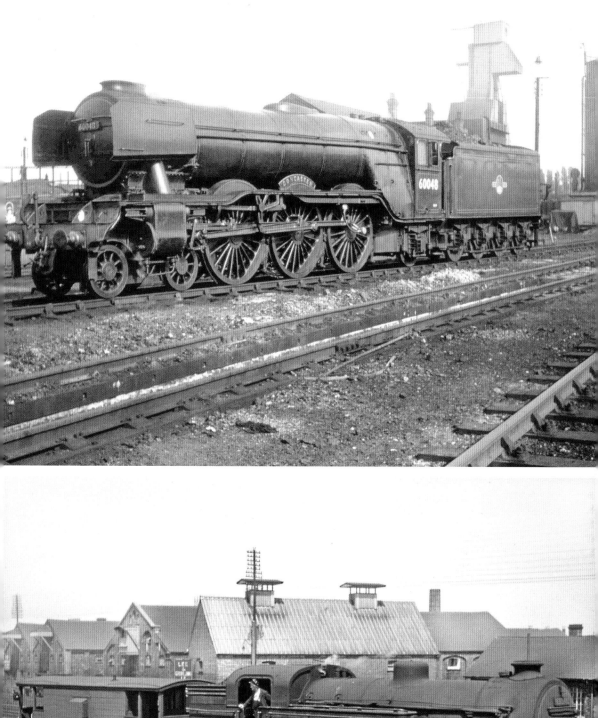

Above GREAT PONTON

Around three miles south of Grantham at Great Ponton, Robinson O4 Class 2-8-0 no. 63606 has a train of mineral wagons, c. 1960. Built at Gorton Works in July 1913, the locomotive has subsequently acquired a diagram 100A boiler and side window cab. No. 63606 was Frodingham-allocated from 1946 until condemned for scrap in June 1965. Photograph by Bill Reed.

Below GREAT PONTON

Another Robinson design caught at Great Ponton was A5 (GCR 9N) Class 4-6-2T no. 69814. The engine is likely seen in mid-1959 when coming to the end of a Grantham allocation. No. 69814 only managed to survive until the end of 1960 when withdrawn from Colwick. Photograph by Bill Reed.

Above GREAT PONTON

The fitting of Kylchap blastpipes and chimneys in the late 1950s gave the Gresley A3s a 'second wind', though accelerating diesel introductions cut short improvements to steam services. No. 60049 *Galtee More* received the equipment in March 1959 and is pictured here just over two years later with an express at Great Ponton. Photograph by Bill Reed.

Below GREAT PONTON

Gresley V2 Class 2-6-2 no. 60977 has a short express freight at Great Ponton on 16th May 1961. Several classmembers had sole allocations to York depot, though V2s with associations to just one depot elsewhere was quite rare. The locomotive was taken out of service from York in February 1962. Photograph by Bill Reed.

Above GUNTHORPE CROSSING

An eastbound freight is on the Leicester-Peterborough line at Gunthorpe crossing – between Oakham and Manton stations – on 26th May 1953. The line was the product of the Midland Railway, leaving the main line north of Leicester at Syston and curving north east to Melton Mowbray. From there the route went southward to Manton before turning eastward to Spalding and reaching Peterborough. The line was built in sections and open throughout from 1848. Several branches were later connected, though most have now disappeared, whilst the main line serves as a cross-country route between Birmingham and Peterborough. Fowler 4F Class no. 44156 of Coalville shed is at the head of the train. Photograph from the Dave Cobbe Collection courtesy Rail Photoprints.

Opposite above HIGH DYKE

Gresley K3 Class 2-6-0 no. 61810 has been guided into the up goods loop at High Dyke, south of Great Ponton, to allow approaching 'Deltic' diesel-electric locomotive D9012 *Crepello* to proceed southward with 'Flying Scotsman' on 16th September 1961. The line was originally two tracks at this point until the up goods line was extended in 1882 from Great Ponton to Stoke Tunnel, whilst the down goods line (far left) was likely installed as part of the High Dyke ironstone branch during the early 20th century. No. 61810 was a Colwick engine at the time of this picture, though a move to Peterborough New England soon occurred. Photograph by Hugh Ballantyne courtesy Rail Photoprints.

Opposite below HIGH DYKE

Around the time of the First World War, the GNR planned a branch south of Great Ponton, running south west to ironstone quarries in the area. This was completed during the conflict and likely in use, though the official date of opening was 1919. Due to the time of completion, with lack of materials and manpower, the line was laid across difficult ground in some places resulting in restrictions on length of trains. This led to sections being assembled in sidings alongside the East Coast Main Line and these are visible here ready to be collected. Gresley V2 Class no. 60881 is about to disappear into Stoke Tunnel with the 09.33 Whitby to King's Cross train on 19th August 1961. Photograph by Hugh Ballantyne courtesy Rail Photoprints.

Above HIGHAM FERRERS STATION

View northward at Higham Ferrers station on 28th May 1959. BR Standard Class 2 2-6-2T no. 84006 has arrived with a local service and prepares to make the return in reverse, being fitted for push-and-pull working. The locomotive had been transferred from Burton to Wellingborough at the start of the year to be used on local duties, one being the Higham branch train. This line left the MR's Wellingborough to Bedford route and was opened in mid-1894. No. 84006 was only employed for a brief period on this task due to the line closing by mid-June 1959. The locomotive continued to be employed in the East Midlands, also at Neasden briefly, until withdrawn in October 1965. Photograph courtesy Rail-Online.

Opposite above HEANOR — BAILEY BROOK SHEDS

Sunk in 1847, Bailey Brook Colliery – on the north side of Heanor – was operational until 1938 when production was concentrated on the nearby Ormonde Colliery. Engine sheds at the aforementioned colliery continued to be used and B.C. 29 is pictured there c. 1960. The locomotive was constructed by Peckett & Sons in 1944 and delivered new to the Butterley Co. which operated two of three pits in the area. B.C. 29 was operational until late 1963 when scrapped on site. Photograph by Bill Reed.

Opposite below HUTHWAITE — NEW HUCKNALL COLLIERY

New Hucknall Colliery was located to the south of Huthwaite, west of Sutton-in-Ashfield, and began production during the late 1870s, continuing until the early 1980s. The colliery was served by both the GNR's Derbyshire and Staffordshire extension and the MR's Blackwell Branch, which also served the nearby Blackwell Colliery. *Swanwick Collieries No. 5* is between duties at New Hucknall Colliery in June 1970. Arriving from Swanwick Colliery in 1961, the engine was scrapped on site 11 years later. Peckett & Sons had constructed *Swanwick Collieries No. 5* in 1940. Photograph by Bill Reed.

Opposite above ILKESTON

Just north of Ilkeston station, Johnson 3F Class no. 43468 has an up coal train in 1954. In the background is Bennerley viaduct which carried the GNR's Derbyshire Extension line over the MR's Erewash Valley route (Long Eaton to Clay Cross). The structure, which stood 60 ft above the valley, was unusually made from lattice ironwork in order to prevent subsidence problems in the heavily mined area. Though the line has now closed, the viaduct stands and is set to be turned into a public walkway. Photograph courtesy Rail-Online.

Opposite below IRCHESTER IRONSTONE QUARRY

Two Irchester Ironstone Quarry locomotives are at the weighbridge on 15th September 1965. On the left is Andrew Barclay 0-4-0ST no. 9 and right is Robert Stephenson & Hawthorns 0-4-0ST *Holwell No. 30*. Both were recent additions to the fleet arriving from Cargo Fleet Ironworks and Holwell Ironworks respectively. Photograph by Hugh Ballantyne courtesy Rail Photoprints.

Below ILKESTON — STANTON IRONWORKS

Andrew Barclay Sons & Co. was one of the main suppliers of steam locomotives to Stanton Ironworks in the period 1930-1950, with one of the new arrivals from the company 0-6-0T *Stanton No. 38* (works no. 2273) in 1949. The locomotive is wearing the livery of the Stanton Ironworks Co. Ltd, which was green with black and white bordering. Engine and crew are happy to pose for the camera on 12th July 1957. Photograph courtesy Rail Photoprints.

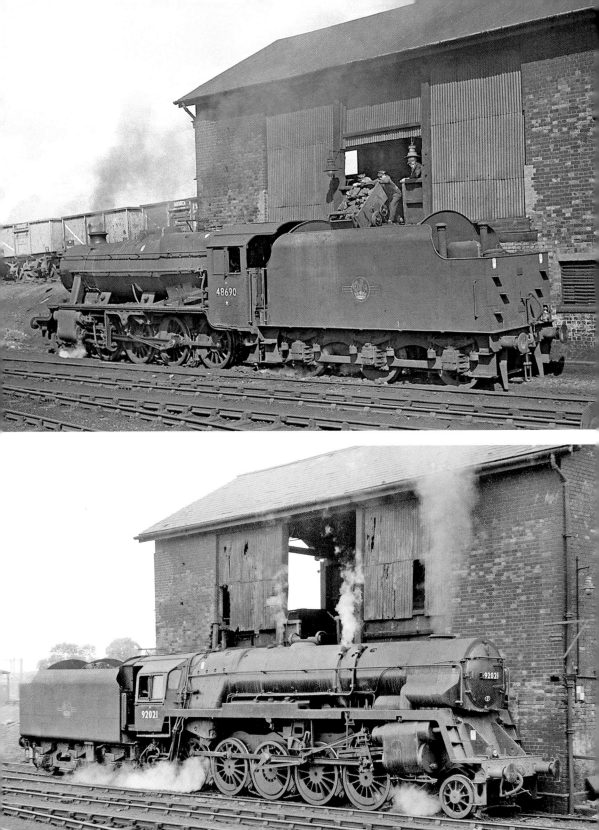

Above KETTERING — COHEN'S SCRAPYARD

George Cohen, Sons & Co. was a well-established firm of scrap merchants (founded in 1834) and one of several such companies that helped British Railways dispose of the large number of steam locomotives becoming redundant in the early 1960s. Despite having several sites across the country, the company – well known as Cohen's – decided to acquire a site in the Midlands to reduce the problem of transporting withdrawn locomotives long distances. In the mid-1960s, Cohen's bought the disused Cransley Ironworks site for disposals to begin, with the first rolling stock arriving in early 1964; these were withdrawn London Transport 'tube' trains, which can be discerned here on the right. Early steam locomotive arrivals were ex-Southern Railway designs – S15 Class 4-6-0s, Q1 Class 0-6-0s and 'Schools' Class 4-4-0s. This image shows an example of the latter class, no. 30921 *Shrewsbury*, with much of the boiler dealt with by the cutting gang by 9th May 1964. The locomotive had been erected at Eastleigh Works in November 1933 and was in service until December 1962, when condemned at Nine Elms depot, London. Cohen's continued to scrap numerous steam locomotives until 1969 and dealt with redundant diesels subsequently. Photograph courtesy Rail-Online.

Opposite above KETTERING SHED

View north east from the platform at Kettering station to the coal stage of Kettering shed. Both of the last two mentioned were built around 1875/1876 and remained in use until the end of steam there in June 1965. Stanier Class 8F no. 48690 is taking coal on 12th April 1963. The locomotive was allocated to the depot at the time and had been since July 1952. No. 48690 moved on before closure, arriving first at Wellingborough in February 1964, then Burton, Westhouses, Colwick and finally Saltley in February 1967 before withdrawal a month later. Photograph by John Briggs courtesy A1 Steam Trust.

Opposite below KETTERING SHED

In contrast to the image opposite above, Kettering shed looks decidedly more dilapidated and evidently some renovation had taken place. BR Standard Class 9F no. 92021 is ready to receive coal in the early 1960s, following a conversion to standard boiler in 1960, having originally the Franco-Crosti boiler. The locomotive was Wellingborough-allocated from new until January 1964, then residing briefly at Kettering. Though increasingly displaced by diesels at this point, the 9Fs at Kettering could see work on main line mineral trains, as well as iron ore trains from local quarries. No. 92021 departed for Carlisle in June 1964 and a year later made a final move to Birkenhead, where withdrawal occurred in November 1967. Photograph from the John Day Collection courtesy Rail Photoprints.

Above KIMBERLEY EAST STATION

Thompson L1 Class 2-6-4T no. 67746 arrives at Kimberley East station with the 13.20 Derby Friargate to Grantham local service on 19th October 1961. Kimberley East was opened on the GNR's Derbyshire and Staffordshire extension in 1876. Photograph by Hugh Ballantyne courtesy Rail Photoprints.

Below KIRKBY-IN-ASHFIELD CENTRAL STATION

A Nottingham Victoria to Mansfield Central local service approaches Kirkby-in-Ashfield Central station in 1955, with Robinson A5 Class no. 69818 leading. Photograph courtesy Rail-Online.

Above LEICESTER BELGRAVE ROAD STATION

The 09.10 express from Leicester to Mablethorpe is at platform 4 ready to depart Leicester Belgrave Road station on 18th August 1962. Thompson B1 Class no. 61177 is at the head of the train. Photograph by John Briggs courtesy A1 Steam Trust.

Below LEICESTER CENTRAL STATION

BR Standard Class 7 'Britannia' Pacific no. 70015 *Apollo* has just detached from a three-coach local all stations service from Nottingham at Leicester Central station on 1st September 1962. Photograph by John Briggs courtesy A1 Steam Trust.

Above LEICESTER LONDON ROAD STATION

On 3rd September 1961, Fowler 3F Class 0-6-0T no. 47502 and crew have a brief respite from station pilot duties at Leicester London Road. The locomotive was Leicester-allocated February 1960 to November 1961. Photograph by John Briggs courtesy A1 Steam Trust.

Below LEICESTER LONDON ROAD STATION

Stanier 'Jubilee' Class no. 45594 *Bhopal* has a northbound express at Leicester London Road station, c. 1950. Opened in 1840, the original station was demolished and the present facility on the Midland main line was built in the early 1890s. Photograph courtesy Rail Photoprints.

Above LEICESTER SHED

View north east from Leicester London Road station to the locomotive depot in 1963. The shed had been extensively rebuilt shortly after the war, including the installation of a trio of coal hoppers that dominate the yard. Closing in 1966, much of the site was cleared, though remains in railway use today. Photograph by John Briggs courtesy A1 Steam Trust.

Below LEICESTER FOREST EAST

On the Burton-on-Trent to Leicester line at Leicester Forest East is a local service on 7th July 1962. Interestingly, the six-coach train is double-headed, using Fowler 4P Class 2-6-4T no. 42331 and Stanier Class 5 4-6-0 no. 44815. Photograph by John Briggs courtesy A1 Steam Trust.

Above LEICESTER CENTRAL STATION

Opened in 1899 on the GCR's London Extension, Leicester Central had a disappointingly short lifespan, closing to express services in 1966, then local traffic in 1969. The site has since been cleared. Stanier Class 5 no. 44938 has a local service at Leicester in 1963. Photograph courtesy Rail Photoprints.

Below LEICESTER

View northward in the direction of Leicester London Road station from Welford Road bridge over the main lines on 16th March 1963 and Fowler 4F Class 0-6-0 no. 44574 is travelling southward light engine. Photograph by John Briggs courtesy A1 Steam Trust.

Above LINCOLN CENTRAL STATION

A southbound express leaves Lincoln Central station behind Thompson B1 Class 4-6-0 no. 61326 on 21st May 1956. The engine was Doncaster-allocated from June 1954 to March 1966 when sent for scrap. Photograph by B.W.L. Brooksbank.

Below LINCOLN CENTRAL STATION

The road users on the right were likely pleased to see the back of Pelham Street crossing (immediately south of Lincoln Central station) when the over bridge was subsequently installed. Here, on 21st May 1956, a Cleethorpes-bound excursion departs behind Gresley J39 no. 64898. Photograph by B.W.L. Brooksbank.

Above LINCOLN PYEWIPE JUNCTION

The Great Northern Railway reached Lincoln with the opening of the Lincolnshire Loop from Peterborough, via Boston and Spalding, in 1848. The company later forged an alliance with the Great Eastern Railway in the early 1880s to build a line from Sleaford, Spalding and March, as well as the wider GER network, allowing for distribution of South Yorkshire's industrial products. The joint line reached the original GNR station, in addition to bypassing Lincoln to the south, then proceeding northward to Gainsborough and Doncaster. Pyewipe Junction was the point the avoiding line joined the tracks from Lincoln station and was later the point for establishing a goods yard and engine shed; the Lancashire, Derbyshire & East Coast Railway line from Chesterfield also later arrived at this point. Robinson D11 (GCR 11F) Class 4-4-0 no. 62669 *Ypres* is approaching Lincoln near Pyewipe Junction with an express from Sheffield Victoria to Cleethorpes, between 1958 and 1960. The engine was based at Sheffield Darnall depot at this time and was withdrawn there in August 1960. Photograph by Bill Reed.

Opposite above LINCOLN ST MARKS STATION

The Great Northern Railway was beaten to Lincoln two years earlier by the Midland Railway with the opening of the line from Nottingham. St Marks station was originally a terminus, though connections were later made with the GNR and GCR to allow transfers of trains. The station was open to traffic until 1985 when services concentrated at Lincoln Central. Thankfully, the station building has been preserved. Robinson D11 Class 4-4-0 no. 62667 *Somme* departs from St Marks station on 13th January 1954 with the 15.08 service to Nottingham. The locomotive had recently transferred to Lincoln from Mexborough and spent around three years in service at the depot. Photograph by R.O. Tuck from Rail Archive Stephenson courtesy Rail-Online.

Opposite below LINCOLN CENTRAL STATION

Light engine at the west end of Lincoln Central, in the early 1960s, is Thompson B1 no. 61026 *Ourebi*. Constructed at Darlington in April 1947, the locomotive's career lasted until February 1966. Five years work at Lincoln took place over this time over two spells – November 1957-November 1959 and March 1960-September 1963. Photograph courtesy Rail-Online.

Above LINCOLN CENTRAL STATION

One of the first long-distance cross-country services to be established in 1885, the 'North Country Continental' ran from Liverpool to Harwich. The train is just starting from the stop at Lincoln on 1st June 1957, with Gresley B17 Class 4-6-0 no. 61645 *The Suffolk Regiment* at the head. Photograph by J.P. Wilson from Rail Archive Stephenson courtesy Rail-Online.

Below LINCOLN CENTRAL STATION

The 'Flying Scotsman' has been diverted from the main line on 1st June 1957, with Gresley A4 Class Pacific no. 60025 *Falcon* bringing the train into Lincoln Central. Photograph by J.P. Wilson from Rail Archive Stephenson courtesy Rail-Online.

Above LINCOLN CENTRAL STATION

Another diverted express is at Lincoln Central station on 1st June 1957. Peppercorn A1 no. 60123 *H.A. Ivatt* has a King's Cross to Leeds and Bradford train. Photograph by J.P. Wilson from Rail Archive Stephenson courtesy Rail-Online.

Below LINCOLN CENTRAL STATION

Robinson A5 Class no. 69828 crosses the River Witham just west of Lincoln Central station with a westbound train, c. 1955. Photograph by J.P. Wilson from Rail Archive Stephenson courtesy Rail-Online.

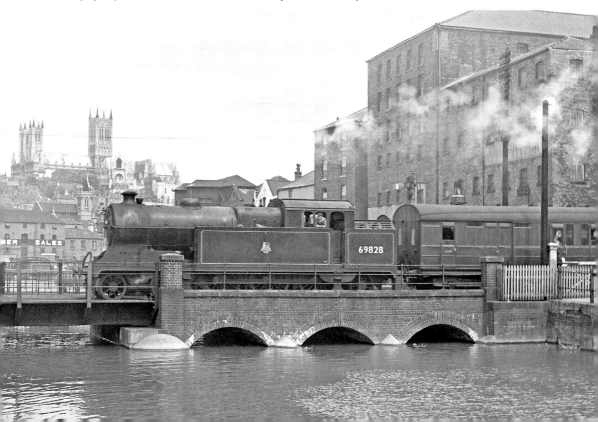

Above LOUGHBOROUGH MIDLAND STATION

View south east from Loughborough Midland station to the ex-Great Central main line over bridge, which has BR Standard Class 5 4-6-0 no. 73010 passing over the Midland main line with a Portsmouth to Nottingham Victoria express on 10th August 1963. Photograph by T.G. Hepburn from Rail Archive Stephenson courtesy Rail-Online.

Below LOUGHBOROUGH

On the other side of the ex-GCR main line bridge looking back to Loughborough Midland station on 6th October 1950, Stanier 'Jubilee' Class 4-6-0 no. 45665 *Lord Rutherford of Nelson* has the 13.25 express from Nottingham Midland to St Pancras. London-allocated at this time, the locomotive moved to Scotland in 1952 and remained there until withdrawn 10 years later. Photograph by B.W.L. Brooksbank.

Above MABLETHORPE STATION

An express arrives at Mablethorpe station behind Colwick B1 no. 61264 during the early 1960s. The station was open from 1877 until forced to close in 1970, despite protracted attempts to keep passenger services. Photograph courtesy Rail-Online.

Below LOUGHBOROUGH

Bedford-allocated Fowler 4F no. 43910 travels southward with a coal train at Loughborough on 6th October 1950. Photograph by B.W.L. Brooksbank.

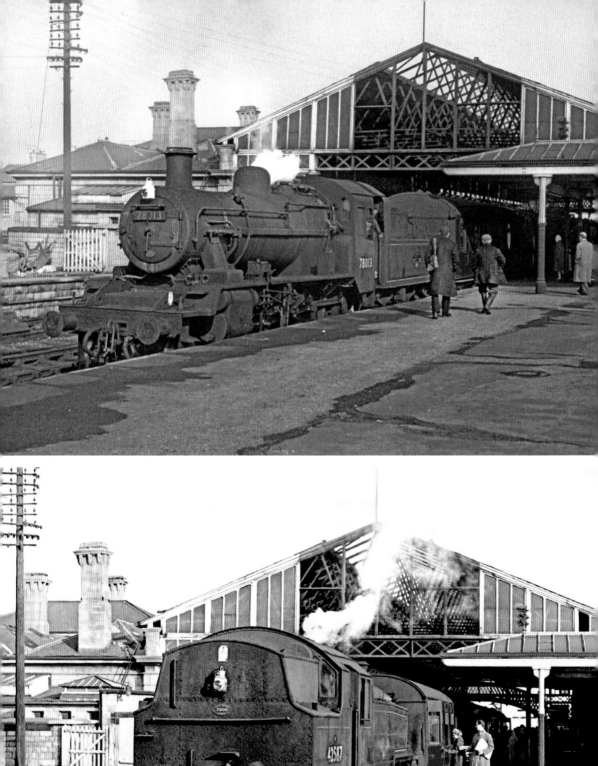

Above MANSFIELD CENTRAL STATION

Despite the presence of the Midland Railway, the Mansfield Railway was promoted in the early 20th century to better serve local colliery interests. Running between the Chesterfield-Lincoln line at Clipstone and GCR main line at Kirkby-in-Ashfield, the railway was opened fully in 1916 and solely operated by the GCR. Three stations were built, including Mansfield Central, and services were mainly between Mansfield and Nottingham, although some did connect with the Chesterfield-Lincoln line at Edwinstowe. Here, on 3rd December 1955, Robinson A5 Class no. 69810 has the 14.24 Mansfield to Nottingham train. Just less than a month remained for passenger services on the line, although collieries continued to be served until the late 20th century. Photograph by T.G. Hepburn from Rail Archive Stephenson courtesy Rail-Online.

Opposite above MANSFIELD TOWN STATION

Passengers prepare to join a local service, perhaps to Nottingham, at Mansfield station on 2nd March 1963. BR Standard Class 2 2-6-0 no. 78013 is at the head of the train and was allocated to Kirkby-in-Ashfield at this time, though moved on to Nottingham at the end of the month. Photograph by Geoff Warnes.

Opposite below MANSFIELD TOWN STATION

Mansfield had an early horse-drawn railway that opened in 1819 and this was later bought by the Midland Railway, which established a passenger station in 1849. This was a terminus, though later became a through route with the opening of the connection between the Nottingham-Lincoln line in the early 1870s, then the extension to Worksop in the middle of the decade. Mansfield station closed in 1964 only to re-open in 1995 as the route between Nottingham and Worksop was re-established and finally completed in 1998. Stanier 4P Class 2-6-4T no. 42587 has another local service at Mansfield station, though has been pictured later on 7th December 1963. The locomotive was another Kirkby-in-Ashfield resident, having left Nottingham in July 1963. No. 42587 was in service until June 1967 and had spells in Wigan, Birkenhead and Bradford before this date. Photograph by Neville Simms from the Ranwell Collection courtesy Rail Photoprints.

Above MARKET HARBOROUGH STATION
Stanier Class 5 no. 44831 departs from Market Harborough station with the 12.29 train from Portsmouth Harbour to Loughborough on 17th July 1965. Photograph by Ian Turnbull courtesy Rail Photoprints.

Below MELBOURNE STATION
Fowler 4F no. 44087 pauses at Melbourne station whilst the tablet is exchanged for a jug of hot water, around 1956. Photograph courtesy Rail Photoprints.

Above MILLERS DALE STATION
A westbound express is at Millers Dale station during the early 1960s, with Stanier 'Jubilee' Class no. 45674 *Duncan* of Saltley shed leading. Photograph by Alan H. Bryant courtesy Rail Photoprints.

Below MILLERS DALE STATION
BR Standard Class 9F no. 92113 has a short freight train at Millers Dale station, around 1963. Photograph by Alan H. Bryant courtesy Rail Photoprints.

Above MELTON MOWBRAY NORTH STATION
A special for Mablethorpe is passing through Melton Mowbray North station behind Thompson B1 no. 61177 on 18th August 1962. Photograph by John Briggs courtesy A1 Steam Trust.

Below MELTON MOWBRAY TOWN STATION
Stanier Class 5 no. 44816 has a Derby to Cromer express at Melton Mowbray Town station on 18th August 1962. Photograph by John Briggs courtesy A1 Steam Trust.

Above MELTON MOWBRAY — HOLWELL IRONWORKS
Hudswell Clark 0-4-0ST *Holwell No. 15* takes on water at Holwell Ironworks in the mid-1950s. Built in 1917 as works no. 1321, the engine was later rebuilt in 1950 and scrapped at Holwell in 1971. Photograph courtesy Rail Photoprints.

Below MUSKHAM TROUGHS
In July 1958 Thompson B1 Class no. 61389 creates a splash taking on water at Muskham troughs whilst working a short train. Photograph by Bill Reed.

Above MUSKHAM TROUGHS

In 1860, the LNWR was the first company to pioneer the use of water troughs for collecting water into the tender without stopping. This was done in an effort to save time as part of an improvement of the 'Irish Mail' train and the first set was installed at Mochdre between Chester and Holyhead. Whilst the LNWR increased the number of troughs in use, the idea was slow to be embraced by other companies and not until the turn of the century did the other railways add troughs to their respective networks. The LNER had six sets on the East Coast Main line. Four were on the ex-Great Northern Railway section – Langley, Werrington, Muskham and Scrooby – whilst two belonged to the ex-North Eastern Railway section – Wiske and Lucker. Here, at Muskham troughs (north of Newark), BR Standard Class 9F no. 92193 is taking water during May 1958. The troughs were over 2,000 feet long and an engine travelling around 60 mph could add 2,000 gallons to the tender in just less than 20 seconds. Photograph by Bill Reed.

Opposite above NEWARK CASTLE STATION

On the Nottingham to Lincoln line, Newark Castle station was opened by the Midland Railway in 1846 and continues to serve passengers. Robinson A5 Class no. 69821 is light engine at the station during the late 1950s. BR Class 10 diesel electric shunter D3615 is on the right and was delivered new to Retford in 1958. Photograph by Bill Reed.

Opposite below NEWARK CASTLE STATION

Fowler 4F no. 44585 is at Newark Castle station in the late 1950s with a freight service. Entering traffic from Derby Works in July 1939, the locomotive was working in Bath at Nationalisation, then moved to Nottingham at the start of the 1950s. The remainder of the decade was spent at the depot and withdrawal occurred in August 1960. Photograph by Bill Reed.

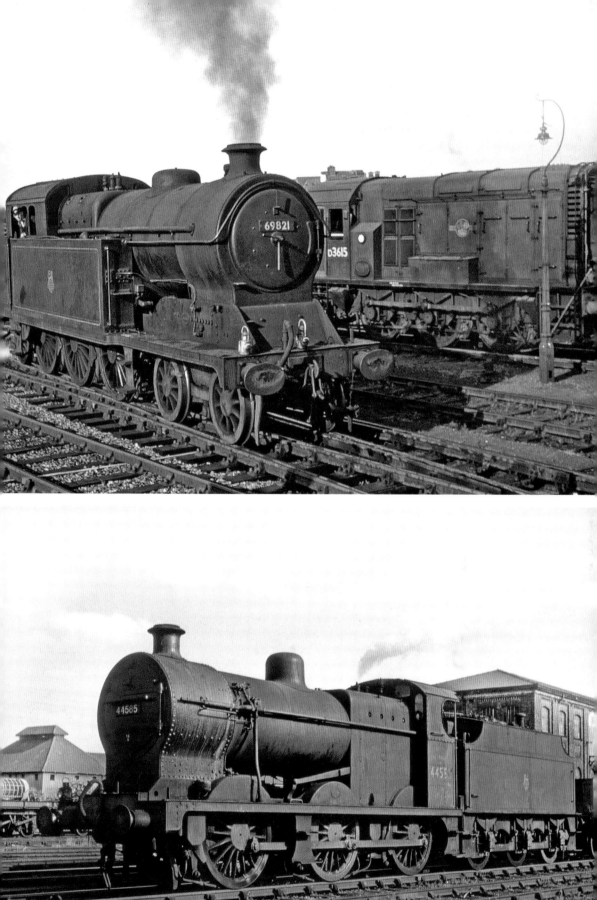

Above NORTHAMPTON

Just after the Second World War, H.G. Ivatt decided to develop Stanier's Class 5 design in order to improve maintenance practices and reliability. One feature introduced on 20 locomotives was poppet valves and Caprotti rotary cam valve gear. This had distinct advantages over piston valves, such as a much reduced rate of wear and greater accuracy when setting valve events. Though successful, and perpetuated on some BR Standard Class 5s, the valves and valve gear did not see widespread use, especially with the onset of dieselisation. Class 5 no. 44744 was built at Crewe Works in July 1948 and was Caprotti-fitted to withdrawal in November 1963. The engine is shunting at Northampton in late July 1963. Photograph courtesy Rail Photoprints.

Opposite above NEWARK NORTH GATE STATION

The Great Northern Railway opened Newark North Gate station in 1852. Serving trains on the main line originally, the station later offered a connection with the GNR and LNWR joint line to Market Harborough and there was also a branch to Leicester. Newark has since lost much of these trains, though a connection has been made with the old MR line to Lincoln. Gresley V2 Class no. 60870 speeds through Newark North Gate with an express freight on 2nd March 1963. Photograph by Geoff Warnes.

Opposite below NEWARK NORTH GATE STATION

Gresley V2 Class no. 60902 has a freight train at Newark North Gate station on 2nd March 1963. The locomotive was erected at Darlington Works in March 1940, starting work from Doncaster depot. After several moves, no. 60902 was withdrawn from Doncaster in September 1963. Photograph by Geoff Warnes.

Opposite above NOTTINGHAM VICTORIA STATION
Robinson D11 Class 4-4-0 no. 62668 *Jutland* is departing Nottingham Victoria station on 24th May 1958, with a bogie milk van coupled to the tender. The locomotive was Manchester-allocated at this time, though transferred to Sheffield in June. Photograph by Geoff Warnes.

Opposite below NORTHAMPTON SHED
Ivatt Class 2MT 2-6-2T no. 41219 is outside the shed at Northampton on 30th July 1963. Fitted with push-and-pull equipment, the locomotive worked at Northampton between March 1962 and July 1965. Moving to Leicester at that time, the engine was condemned there three months later. Photograph courtesy Rail Photoprints.

Below NOTTINGHAM ARKWRIGHT STREET STATION
As the GCR progressed with the London Extension, Nottingham Arkwright Street station was opened in 1899, though was later superseded by Victoria as the main station in the city. Arkwright Street was closer to the Midland Railway station, allowing for transfer of passengers to that line, also, as the sign suggests here, for visitors to the football and cricket grounds. An unusual engine pictured at the station on 22nd June 1948 is Hawksworth 'Modified Hall' 4-6-0 no. 6990 *Witherslack Hall*, which is working the 10.00 London Marylebone to Manchester London Road express as part of the 1948 'Locomotive Exchanges'. Photograph by J.P. Wilson from Rail Archive Stephenson courtesy Rail-Online.

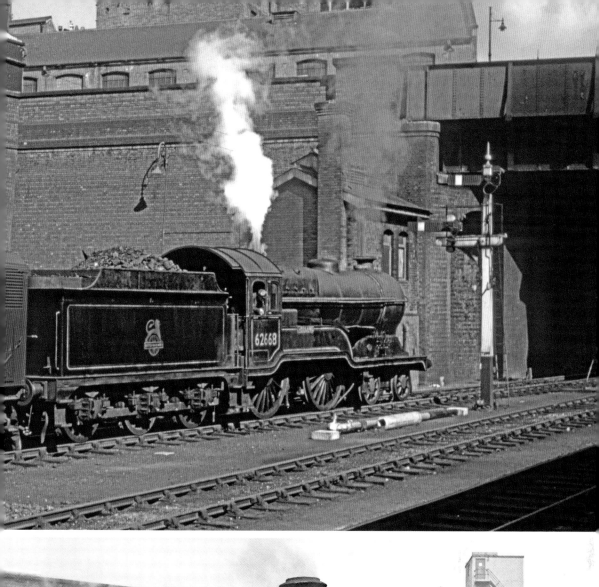

Above NOTTINGHAM MIDLAND STATION

A pair of Fairburn 4P Class 2-6-4T locomotives – no. 42089 and no. 42218 – is at Nottingham Midland station on 10th October 1964. This was the last day of traffic on the Nottingham to Worksop line and these engines, being allocated to Kirkby-in-Ashfield, were likely working the final trains. Photograph by Geoff Warnes.

Below NOTTINGHAM MIDLAND STATION

The 14.30 local to Chesterfield is at Nottingham Midland station on 22nd May 1957, with BR Standard Class 4 no. 75059 the motive power. Photograph by J.P. Wilson from Rail Archive Stephenson courtesy Rail-Online.

Above NOTTINGHAM MIDLAND STATION

Holden D16/3 (rebuilt from D15) Class 4-4-0 no. 62599 arrives at Nottingham Midland station with a local train from Lincoln in the late 1950s. Several class members were drafted to take over the services on the Midland route in early 1957 and performed well to late 1958 as DMUs were given preference. No. 62599 survived until September 1958 when condemned. Photograph courtesy Rail-Online.

Below NOTTINGHAM VICTORIA STATION

On 25th September 1957, Gresley J6 Class 0-6-0 no. 64215 takes on water from a platform column at Nottingham Victoria station. Opened in May 1900, the station was a considerable undertaking, covering 13 acres and possessing two large island platforms measuring nearly 1,300 ft in length. Deemed superfluous to the operations of BR, the GCR's London Extension was run down in the 1960s and Nottingham Victoria closed in September 1967 and the site cleared for the erection of a shopping centre. Photograph by Bill Reed.

Above OAKHAM STATION
A Derby to Kettering train is at Oakham station on 25th May 1953, with Fowler 4P Compound 4-4-0 no. 41053 leading. Photograph from Dave Cobbe Collection courtesy Rail Photoprints.

Below OAKHAM STATION
Ivatt Class 2 2-6-0 no. 46403 has a local service at Oakham station on 25th May 1953. Photograph from Dave Cobbe Collection courtesy Rail Photoprints.

Above PINXTON — BROOKHILL COLLIERY
Andrew Barclay 0-4-0ST, works no. 905, is at Brookhill Colliery, Pinxton, c. 1960. The locomotive arrived in 1949 and was used to 1966. Photograph by Bill Reed.

Below PINXTON — BROOKHILL COKING PLANT
Andrew Barclay 0-4-0ST *Burdale*, works no. 973, is at Brookhill Coking Plant, Pinxton, around 1960. Transported to the site during demolition of the plant, the locomotive was not steamed and later scrapped there. Photograph by Bill Reed.

Above PEAK FOREST STATION

The area around Buxton in the Peak District consists of a limestone outcrop. With this mineral being an important constituent of building materials from at least the time of the Ancient Egyptians, quarrying naturally followed. This was done in the Peak District from Roman times, though intensified during the Industrial Revolution. The construction of the Midland Railway line through the area allowed greater exploitation and this continues to the present. At Peak Forest station with a southbound freight – including empty mineral hoppers – during June 1962 is BR Standard Class 9F no. 92018 and Fowler 4F Class no. 44419. Both were Rowsley-allocated at this time, though no. 44419 was soon to transfer to Saltley depot. Peak Forest station was opened in 1867 and served traffic until 1967. The building still stands and is used by a quarrying company. Photograph by A.E. Durrant courtesy Rail Photoprints.

Opposite above RADFORD STATION

Stanier 3P Class 2-6-2T no. 40073 moves off from the platform at Radford station with a local service from Nottingham to Kirkby-in-Ashfield during March 1960. The engine was an early example of the class, being erected as part of the first batch at Derby Works in February 1935. With a varied allocation history under BR, no. 40073 had spells in London, the Midlands and Wales, settling at Kirkby-in-Ashfield for the final two years in service, being condemned for scrap in August 1962. Radford station would also close in 1964 after 116 years. Photograph by Dave Swale courtesy Rail Photoprints.

Opposite below RATCLIFFE-ON-SOAR

The coal trains between Toton and Brent Sidings were an institution on the Midland Main Line and worked by a variety of motive power. Here, on 18th June 1957, BR Standard Class 9F no. 92026 has such a service at Ratcliffe-on-Soar (south of Trent Junction). Equipped with the Franco-Crosti boiler, the locomotive only used the conventional chimney when lighting-up and the side exhaust was the main chimney. This could make the cab a very unpleasant place and contributed to the conversion of the engines so equipped. Photograph by T.G. Hepburn from Rail Archive Stephenson courtesy Rail-Online.

Above RETFORD STATION

Introduced for mixed duties in the North East and East of England, the Peppercorn K1 Class 2-6-0 was produced in 1949 and 1950, with 70 locomotives completed. No. 62037 was built at the North British Locomotive Company's works, Glasgow, and dispatched to March shed in September 1949. The engine spent 12 years there before moving to Retford GC shed, finding work mostly on local and medium distance freight services. No. 62037 has been pressed into passenger service here, having an excursion at Retford station on 29th July 1962. Transferring to Doncaster in November of that year, and being used on similar duties, the locomotive was withdrawn in December 1964. Photograph by Geoff Warnes.

Opposite RETFORD GC SHED

The Great Central Railway established a locomotive depot to the east of Retford station in 1849. This was a three-road building, with associated facilities, and remained in use, relatively unchanged (apart from a new roof), until closed in 1965. Under British Railways, the shed had around 60 locomotives on the roster and these were mainly freight types. In the congested shed yard on Sunday, 17th June 1962, many examples of these are seen, with two identifiable by number. On the left, reposing on the shear legs road, is Gresley K3 Class 2-6-0 no. 61951. The locomotive was erected by the North British Locomotive Company, Glasgow, during October 1935 and in service until November 1962. No. 61951 was allocated to Doncaster when pictured. To the right is classmate no. 61812 which was the product of Darlington Works in August 1924, lasting in traffic until September 1962. The engine was also a Doncaster resident. Photograph by Geoff Warnes.

Above RETFORD

A northbound express travels away from Retford station on 15th July 1961. Gresley V2 Class 2-6-2 no. 60866 is leading and had recently transferred from Doncaster to Grantham. Photograph by Geoff Warnes.

Opposite above RETFORD STATION

The Manchester, Sheffield & Lincolnshire Railway's Sheffield-Gainsborough route was the first to pass through Retford in 1849, though quickly joined by Great Northern Railway's line from Doncaster. The MS&LR had built a station and this was used by both lines until the completion of the Peterborough to Doncaster or 'Towns Line' in 1852 when a new station was built serving both railways. The two routes crossed just to the south of the station and this could be disadvantageous, which led to the construction of the Retford 'dive under' in the mid-1960s. Long-term Retford GC shed resident B1 no. 61212 has a southbound local service at Retford on 29th September 1962. Photograph courtesy Rail-Online.

Opposite below RETFORD STATION

Peppercorn A1 Class Pacific no. 60118 *Archibald Sturrock* is at Retford station with the 12.03 Leeds to King's Cross express on 1st July 1961. The locomotive was built at Doncaster Works in November 1948, though was nameless at this time. In mid-1950, no. 60118 was bestowed with the name of the Great Northern Railway's first Locomotive Engineer, 1850-1866. New to Copley Hill depot, Leeds, the engine was in the city until condemned in October 1965, though had moved on to Ardsley, then Neville Hill in the 1960s. Photograph courtesy Rail Photoprints.

Above RETFORD GN SHED

Another member of the Gresley O2 Class contingent at Retford was no. 63926 and the engine is pictured at the GN shed, c. 1960. Part of the first 11 built by the GNR, the locomotive entered traffic in June 1921 and featured slight detail differences from pioneer, no. 461, being Class O2/1. Later, the engines in this subcategory had side-window cabs fitted, with no. 63926 being a recipient in October 1940. The locomotive also received a diagram 100A boiler in March 1961, being amongst the last conversions; this change is yet to take place. Photograph by Bill Reed.

Opposite above RETFORD STATION

A northbound partially-fitted freight passes Retford South signal box on 17th October 1963. The line curving off to the left is joining the Sheffield-Gainsborough route, which is just behind the tender of the locomotive and the point where the railwayman is crossing. Gresley A3 Class Pacific no. 60106 *Flying Fox* is the engine in charge and was coming to the end of a long career at this time. Built at Doncaster Works in April 1923 as part of the first ten A1s constructed, the locomotive was later reboilered and reclassified A3 in March 1947. Mainly working on the ECML, *Flying Fox* did have a spell on the ex-GC main line in the mid-1950s. By 1963, the engine had been displaced to Peterborough New England depot, which focussed on freight, and withdrawal from there took place in December 1964. Photograph courtesy Rail-Online.

Opposite below RETFORD STATION

Just as the Robinson 2-8-0 was adopted by the ROD in the First World War, a simplified version of Stanier's 8F was built for the War Department in World War Two. Some 935 'Austerity' locomotives were completed between 1943 and 1945 and 733 would be purchased following the conflict, with the LNER taking 200 and British Railways the remainder. No. 90001 was erected by the North British Locomotive Company at Hyde Park Works in February 1943 and was later taken into stock by the LNER in late 1946. The engine worked initially in the North East before moving southward. When pictured at Retford station on 17th October 1963, no. 90001 was a Doncaster engine. Photograph courtesy Rail-Online.

Above RETFORD GC SHED

On Sunday, 14th July 1957, a number of locomotives are at rest in Retford GC shed yard. In the foreground is Robinson J11/4 (GCR 9J) Class 0-6-0 no. 64421, whilst to the right is Gresley J39 Class 0-6-0 no. 64830 and on the extreme left is WD 'Austerity' Class 2-8-0 no. 90252. Both the J11/4 and J39 were Retford engines, with no. 90252 based at Mexborough. Photograph by Bill Reed.

Opposite below RETFORD STATION

Thompson A2/2 Class Pacific no. 60502 *Earl Marischal* arrives at Retford station with a parcels service on 23rd May 1961. Rebuilt from Gresley's P2 Class in June 1944, the engine ran as A2/2 until condemned in July 1961 as the last of the six-member class still in service. No. 60502 was York-allocated for much of the BR period. Photograph courtesy Rail-Online.

Above RETFORD STATION

Constructed at Doncaster in March 1937, Gresley A4 Class Pacific no. 60028 *Walter K. Whigham* was coming to the end of a career spanning 25 years when pictured with an express at Retford station on 29th September 1962. The locomotive had started life as no. 4487 *Sea Eagle* and was rechristened in October 1947 to honour the Deputy Chairman of the LNER from 1946-1948, being one of several such changes honouring servants of the company. Photograph courtesy Rail-Online.

Above RETFORD

View west at Retford as Robinson D11 Class 4-4-0 no. 62662 *Prince of Wales* comes off the Sheffield to Lincoln line on to the curve providing access to Retford station with a local train during September 1959. The locomotive was a recent addition to those used at Sheffield Darnall shed and was withdrawn from there in August 1960. Photograph by Geoff Warnes.

Opposite above ROADE

BR Standard Class 5 4-6-0 no. 73020 is on the West Coast Main Line at Roade with a southbound express from Northampton to Euston on 22nd July 1953. The locomotive had entered traffic from Derby Works in October 1951 and sent to Chester. From there, the engine was to move on to Shrewsbury, Swindon, Weymouth and Guildford before withdrawal in July 1967. Photograph courtesy Rail Photoprints.

Opposite below RUDDINGTON

South of Nottingham at Ruddington, on 20th June 1961, is Gresley J39 Class 0-6-0 no. 64749 and the locomotive appears to be running tender-first with a brake van. Constructed at Darlington Works in August 1928, no. 64749 was one of 261 completed there from the class total of 289. From new the locomotive was paired with a Group Standard 3,500-gallon tender with space for 5½ tons of coal; the filler cap appears to be missing and poor quality coal has spilled out of the coal space. No. 64749 was allocated to Ardsley shed from May 1948 to November 1962. Photograph by Bill Reed.

Above RUDDINGTON

BR Standard Class 9F no. 92091 has a train of empty bolster wagons at Ruddington on 20th June 1961. The locomotive was one of a number of 9Fs new to Doncaster depot in late 1956, yet these engines only remained there for a short time. A reorganisation of motive power saw them dispatched to Annesley shed to help facilitate improvements of the intense workings – coal, steel, and goods – to the South and South West of England. Their arrival allowed a general reduction of journey times through increased speed. The 9Fs were in use until the rundown of freight on the ex-GCR main line in 1965. At this time no. 92091 was transferred to Speke Junction, Liverpool, and was withdrawn from Carnforth shortly after arriving in May 1968. Photograph by Bill Reed.

Opposite above RUDDINGTON

View north along the ex-GCR main line from Station Road bridge – now Clifton Road bridge – Ruddington, on 20th June 1961. BR Standard Class 5 no. 73157 is approaching with an express bound for London Marylebone station. Ruddington was provided with a station on the west side of the village as part of the London Extension, opening on 15th March 1899 and in use until 4th March 1963. No. 73157 was new from Doncaster in December 1956 and one of five classmembers allocated at this time to Neasden. After several moves the engine had returned to that depot when pictured, though would leave for Cricklewood in June 1962. The locomotive almost survived to the end of steam and was condemned at Patricroft in May 1968. Photograph by Bill Reed.

Opposite below RUDDINGTON

An early evening fish train from Grimsby is at Ruddington around 1962/1963. The train is led by BR Standard Class 7 'Britannia' Pacific no. 70037 *Hereward the Wake*, which was working from Immingham at this time. The engine had been displaced from East Anglia following the introduction of diesels and arrived at the depot in September 1961 and had just over two years there. Photograph courtesy Rail-Online.

Above SLEAFORD STATION
The Railway Correspondence & Travel Society organised 'The Fensman' railtour for 9th September 1956, taking in much of East Anglia, including the Benwick and Upwell goods branches, which were travelled in open wagons. Gresley K2 Class no. 61743 is ready to work the Sleaford to Spalding portion from the aforementioned station. Photograph by Hugh Ballantyne courtesy Rail Photoprints.

Opposite above SEATON STATION
Ex-London, Tilbury & Southend Railway Whitelegg Class 79 4-4-2T no. 41975 has an Uppingham branch train at Seaton station during 1958. Photograph by Dave Cobbe courtesy Rail Photoprints.

Opposite below SEATON STATION
Ivatt Class 2 2-6-2T no. 41212 is in the bay platform at Seaton station with a local service to Stamford on 16th September 1965. Photograph by Hugh Ballantyne courtesy Rail Photoprints.

Above SLEAFORD STATION

With the close proximity of the GNR line from Peterborough to Boston and Lincoln, local businessmen in Sleaford saw the advantage of connecting with the railway. The Boston, Sleaford & Midland Counties Railway was promoted in the early 1850s to link the then completed Peterborough-Grantham section of the GNR main line at Barkston with Boston on the 'Lincolnshire Loop'. Barkston to Sleaford was the first section completed in mid-1857, followed by the line to Boston in April 1859. The GNR soon moved to formally absorb the company and did so in 1865. Later, the company built a line from Sleaford to Bourne and the GN&GE Joint Line from March passed Sleaford to the east, though a loop was established to connect the routes. Gresley B17 Class no. 61635 *Milton* was March-allocated when pictured at Sleaford station with an express during the 1950s. Photograph courtesy Rail-Online.

Opposite above SKEGNESS STATION

A trip on lines in Nottingham and Lincolnshire was the order of the day on 12th September 1964, being organised by the Railway Correspondence & Travel Society. Stanier Class 5 no. 44918 was the engine throughout and departed from Nottingham Midland in late morning heading for Newark. The train then left the Midland line to join the GN route and travelled southward to Barkston to take the GN line to Lincoln which was scheduled for closure in 1965. At Lincoln, the train went to the Horncastle branch, then closed to passengers for some time but still used for freight, and the first leg ended with a journey to Skegness. No. 44918 is at the station ready to complete the second leg which travelled via Gainsborough, Retford and Worksop to join the Midland line back to Nottingham. Photograph courtesy Rail Photoprints.

Opposite below SLEAFORD JUNCTION

Joining the Boston-Lincoln line with a local train at Sleaford Junction during 1953 is Holden B12 (GER S69) Class 4-6-0 no. 61538. Introduced in 1911 to take over on principal expresses, the class numbered 71 at Grouping, with a further ten ordered in the late 1920s pending the introduction of Gresley's B17 Class 4-6-0. No. 61538 emerged from Stratford Works in July 1915. The locomotive was later one of fifty-five classmembers fitted with an ACFI feedwater heater, receiving the apparatus in December 1932. This was later removed in June 1937 as the results were not satisfactory. A more beneficial improvement was the rebuilding of many B12s with a new boiler, as well as other detail changes, in the early 1930s, with the process continuing until the mid-1940s; no. 61538 was modified in June 1937. The engine survived until January 1957. Photograph courtesy Rail-Online.

Above SPONDON
Gresley K3 Class 2-6-0 no. 61907 is ready to be scrapped at Albert Looms' Scrapyard, Spondon, in January 1964. Photograph courtesy Rail Photoprints.

Opposite above SPALDING STATION
Thompson B1 no. 61073 has a King's Cross to Cleethorpes express at Spalding during the mid-1950s. Photograph courtesy Rail-Online.

Opposite below SPONDON
A local service from Nottingham to Derby is at Spondon (east of Derby) in May 1963 with Hughes 'Crab' Class 2-6-0 no. 42896. Photograph courtesy Rail Photoprints.

Above SPONDON

As mentioned previously, private scrap merchants assisted British Railways in disposing of redundant steam locomotives. Albert Looms at Spondon, near Derby, became involved in the process in 1959 and took a modest number through to 1965. One ready for the breakers in August 1962 is Fowler 4P Class 2-6-4T no. 42383. The locomotive had been constructed at Derby Works in July 1932 and was in service until October 1961, being removed from traffic at Toton shed. Photograph courtesy Rail Photoprints.

Opposite above STAMFORD TOWN STATION

The 09.35 service from Seaton has just arrived at Stamford Town station behind Ivatt Class 2MT 2-6-2T no. 41212 on 16th September 1965. The station was the first to serve Stamford, opening in October 1846 on the Syston & Peterborough Railway line. In the early 1850s, the LNWR made a connection with the line at Luffenham, allowing services to run between Seaton and Stamford. The Stamford & Essendine Railway opened in 1856, providing a link to the GNR main line. The presence of two stations in Stamford resulted in name changes by BR, with the first station becoming Stamford Town and the second Stamford East in 1950, though the latter only survived until 1957. Stamford Town reverted to Stamford in 1966 and continues to serve passengers. Photograph by Hugh Ballantyne courtesy Rail Photoprints.

Opposite below STOKE TUNNEL

Gresley A4 Class Pacific no. 60029 *Woodcock* has just exited Stoke Tunnel with the southbound 'Norseman' express on 19th August 1961. This train was the 12.10 from Tyne Commission Quay to King's Cross which connected with boats to Norway and was reintroduced following the war in 1947, running to 1966. No. 60029 was allocated to King's Cross for much of the engine's career and was withdrawn from Peterborough New England shortly after the aforementioned depot closed to steam. Photograph by Hugh Ballantyne courtesy Rail Photoprints.

Above STAPLEFORD & SANDIACRE STATION
Upon the formation of the London, Midland & Scottish Railway in 1923, the need for a suitable shunting and local freight locomotive was identified. Chief Mechanical Engineer Henry Fowler drew inspiration from Johnson's 2441 Class 0-6-0T, several of which he had recently rebuilt, for his own standard 3F Class 0-6-0T. The first batches appeared in 1924 and a steady stream appeared in traffic up to 1931; interestingly nearly all 422 locomotives came from contractors and not until the last batch was the company's own works (Horwich) involved. No. 47551 was constructed by the Hunslet Engine Co. in January 1928 and was in service until February 1963. The locomotive is shunting at Stapleford & Sandiacre station on 17th May 1962. Photograph by B.W.L. Brooksbank.

Opposite above STAPLEFORD & SANDIACRE STATION
Located a short distance to the north of Toton Marshalling Yard, Stapleford & Sandiacre station witnessed a large number of freight trains daily. One coal train passing southward to the yard on 17th May 1962 is led by WD 'Austerity' Class 2-8-0 no. 90612. The locomotive was erected at Vulcan Foundry in January 1944 and worked the rest of the year for the LNER at Colwick. In 1945, no. 90612, as WD no. 77468, was transferred to Belgium and 18 months elapsed before the locomotive returned to Britain and the LNER took the engine into stock again. After Nationalisation, no. 90612 settled at Mexborough shed and was withdrawn from there in March 1964. Photograph by B.W.L. Brooksbank.

Opposite below STAPLEFORD & SANDIACRE STATION
Located on the Erewash Valley line, Stapleford & Sandiacre station was opened as Sandiacre & Stapleford in September 1847. The facilities were upgraded in the early 1870s and in the following decade the name was switched around, remaining in that form until closed in early 1967. Another coal train is passing through the station on 17th May 1962 and headed by Stanier 8F Class no. 48185. The engine was allocated to Toton throughout the 1950s and was to move on in June 1962 to Nottingham. Photograph by B.W.L. Brooksbank.

Above STAVELEY BARROW HILL SHED

Even though the MR passed through Staveley from the 1840s, stabling facilities were not deemed necessary until 1865 when a four-track shed was built near Staveley station, later renamed Barrow Hill. This was soon superseded by a roundhouse sited to the west and which is still in railway use and maintained by the Barrow Hill Engine Shed Society. Two small sheds were also provided at the Staveley Chemical and Iron Works and the GCR opened a large depot in the early 1890s; all were active to the mid-1960s. Two 0F 0-4-0STs (no. 47005 and no. 47001), a 1F 0-6-0T and a WD 'Austerity' are pictured at Barrow Hill shed – seemingly out of service – in 1965. Photograph courtesy Rail Photoprints.

Opposite above STAVELEY CHEMICAL WORKS

Formed near Chesterfield in the early 1860s, the Staveley Coal & Iron Company started as an ironworks, though later entered new fields, such as mining and chemical production. As a result the company's site (east of Staveley Town) became extensive and shunters were used to move materials and products. Unusually, this was done by locomotives loaned from the MR, LMSR and the London Midland Region of BR. 0F Class 0-4-0ST no. 47005 is at work for the company during 1964. Allocated to nearby Barrow Hill shed as a result of employment at Staveley, this covered the period between June 1963 and October 1965. Photograph courtesy Rail Photoprints.

Opposite below STAVELEY CHEMICAL WORKS

Johnson's 1377 Class (LMSR 1F) 0-6-0T was built between 1878 and 1892, numbering 185 examples. The class survived intact until shortly after grouping and over half had been disposed of by Nationalisation. A small group was retained at Barrow Hill shed for use at Staveley Chemical Works, with one, no. 41739, at work here in 1958. The locomotive was erected at Derby Works in November 1884 and survived until June 1963; the last was condemned in 1965, whilst no. 41708 has been preserved. Photograph courtesy Rail Photoprints.

Above STONEYFORD

Fairburn 4P Class 2-6-4T no. 42185 has a southbound local parcels train at Stoneyford (east of Codnor) on the Erewash Valley line. Pictured on 12th July 1963, the locomotive had just under a year left in service, being condemned during May 1964. Photograph by B.W.L. Brooksbank.

Opposite above STONEYFORD

An express freight is on the northbound goods line at Stoneyford on 12th July 1963. The locomotive is Stanier Class 5 no. 44806 of Nottingham which managed to see the end of steam in August 1968 and was subsequently preserved. Presently, no. 44806 resides on the North Yorkshire Moors Railway. Photograph by B.W.L. Brooksbank.

Opposite below STOREFIELD QUARRY

An ironstone quarry was established at Geddington – between Kettering and Corby – around the turn of the century. This was active until the late 1920s, though in the early 1930s the South Durham Steel & Iron Co. Ltd acquired the mining rights. Operations did not begin until the early 1940s, with the site referred to as Storefield Quarry. The original company had a narrow gauge system, whilst the new owners opted for standard gauge and had several locomotives to shunt the site. One was Andrew Barclay (works no. 2101) no. 19 which arrived in early 1941 and was at work until 1969. The engine has loaded hopper wagons for the exchange sidings on 14th September 1965. Photograph by Hugh Ballantyne courtesy Rail Photoprints.

Above TOTON

Though unidentified, this Beyer Garratt 2-6-0+0-6-2 is likely no. 47998 or no. 47999 due to being unequipped with a rotating coal bunker, as the remaining classmembers had the feature. The locomotive is at Toton Yard with an unfitted express freight in August 1958. Photograph by Bill Reed.

Below TOTON SHED

Ex-LT&SR Whitelegg Class 79 4-4-2T no. 41966 has been displaced to Toton shed and is pictured in front of the water tank on 30th October 1955. Photograph by Bill Reed.

Above TIBSHELF TOWN STATION

On the last day of services at Tibshelf Town station on 2nd March 1963, Fowler 3F Class 0-6-0T no. 47283 is light engine. Photograph by Geoff Warnes.

Below TOTON SHED

Closed officially to steam in December 1965, facilities at Toton appear to have been available to visiting locomotives into early 1966. Two Doncaster-built 8Fs no. 48527 and 48528 (closest to camera) are serviced there with another unidentified classmember on 20th February. Photograph courtesy Rail-Online.

Above TUXFORD SHED

A small depot was established at Tuxford by the Lancashire, Derbyshire & East Coast Railway in 1896. Located near the junction with the GNR's Grantham to Doncaster line, the shed was improved by the GCR in the early 20th century and remained open until 1959. Robinson O4/8 Class 2-8-0 no. 63776 is in the yard at Tuxford during April 1958. Visiting from Langwith Junction, the locomotive survived there until December 1962. Robinson J11 0-6-0 no. 64333 is also partially visible on the left. Allocated to Tuxford at this time, the engine transferred to Langwith Junction on closure of the aforementioned and was withdrawn at the latter during August 1962. Photograph by Ian Turnbull courtesy Rail Photoprints.

Opposite above TOTON SHED

The focal point for coal and freight traffic from Derbyshire, Nottinghamshire and Yorkshire was Toton Marshalling Yard, just north of Trent Junction on the main line. As a result, suitable stabling and servicing facilities were established with the first roundhouse of 1870. Soon after, a second roundhouse was added to the south wall and this was followed by a third, again to the south, in 1901. Stabled inside one of these on 7th October 1962 is Stanier Class 5 no. 44866 of Rugby. Photograph courtesy Rail-Online.

Opposite below TUXFORD

View south at Tuxford as Peppercorn A1 Class Pacific no. 60133 *Pommern* passes Tuxford Junction signal box with the down 'Queen of Scots' Pullman on 10th August 1957. The box controlled the branch between the GNR main line and LD&ECR (later GCR) line between Chesterfield and Lincoln, which has a train passing over the bridge in the background. The 'Queen of Scots' Pullman evolved from the 'Harrogate Pullman' introduced by the LNER in 1923 and was changed in 1928 to extend the journey from Harrogate to Newcastle, Edinburgh and Glasgow. Under BR, the train left King's Cross at 12.00 and took almost 9 hours and 15 minutes to reach Glasgow; a similar schedule was in force for the reverse train. Peppercorn's A1s was the preferred motive power for much of the journey and no. 60133 was a Leeds engine. Photograph by N.E. Preedy courtesy Rail Photoprints.

Above WELLINGBOROUGH SHED

Wellingborough was another part of the East Midlands rich in ironstone deposits and the resulting industry around this was aided by the railways, particularly the Midland Railway which ran along the eastern side of the town. A large locomotive depot was eventually established north of the station, with the first building erected being a roundhouse in 1868. This was followed by a second roundhouse just four years later and finally a two-track shed in 1935. With the focus of the depot on freight traffic, this role dominated the types allocated and around Nationalisation the majority of the engines there were Stanier 8F Class 2-8-0s, with 34 officially there on 1st January. Following the introduction of BR Standard Class 9Fs in the mid-1950s, a number of 8Fs were displaced, though the class continued to be well represented until the depot closed in June 1966. No. 48625 is at Wellingborough shed around 1959/1960 and appears to be out of service. The locomotive had been resident there from 1946 and would transfer to Cricklewood in June 1960. Photograph by Bill Reed.

Opposite WELLINGBOROUGH SHED

The ten Franco-Crosti boilered BR Standard Class 9Fs were concentrated at Wellingborough shed to work on the coal traffic to and from Brent sidings, London. Crews at the depot soon found working with the locomotives to be disagreeable owing to the side-mounted chimney. Despite modifications, the problem was such that conversion to use a standard boiler became the only option. This process became drawn out and the Franco-Crosti engines were often stored out of service at Wellingborough and this is the case here for no. 92021, which covered the period of a year between April 1959 and 1960, with conversion taking place at Crewe Works by June 1960. Photograph by Bill Reed.

Above WELLINGBOROUGH SHED

A scene captured in Wellingborough shed during May 1962 shows three men apparently working with boiler tubes in front of Johnson 1142 (LMSR 2F) Class 0-6-0 no. 58148. The locomotive was visiting from Coalville at this time and was perhaps awaiting attention from the fitters; no. 58148 was last in works for attention during April 1958. Photograph courtesy Rail-Online.

Opposite above WELLINGBOROUGH LONDON ROAD STATION

The London & Birmingham Railway initially bypassed Northampton when opened in 1838 due to engineering issues, yet a branch to the town was soon planned. This was opened in 1845, though had become part of a larger project to connect with Peterborough through the Nene Valley which was completed a very short time later. Wellingborough (London Road added in 1924) station opened at this point to the south of the town and a connection was later made with the Midland line to the north east. Fowler 4F Class no. 44215 has the 16.00 local service from Peterborough East to Northampton on 18th August 1962. Passenger trains were withdrawn from the line in 1964 and freight ceased during 1966, though the line was not abandoned until the early 1970s. The northernmost part of the line west of Peterborough was later taken over and used as part of the Nene Valley Railway. Photograph by B.W.L. Brooksbank.

Opposite below WELLINGBOROUGH LONDON ROAD STATION

Another local service is at Wellingborough London Road station, though the train is coupled to Ivatt Class 2MT 2-6-2T no. 41224 and travelling from Northampton to Peterborough on 30th June 1962. The engine, which is push-pull fitted, was well-travelled and allocation to Wellingborough lasted from March 1962 to January 1963. No. 41224 ended life on the Southern Region and was withdrawn from Bournemouth in July 1967. Photograph courtesy Rail-Online.

Above WEST HALLAM STATION

On the GNR's Derbyshire and Staffordshire Extension line, West Hallam station (just west of Ilkeston) opened on 1st April 1878 and served passengers until 7th September 1964. During this time, the station was also known as West Hallam for Dale Abbey and this is displayed on the sign to the left. On the right is Stanley Colliery, which was not present when the station opened, though had been sunk by the end of the century. Ivatt Class 4MT no. 43032 has the 12.55 Derby Friargate to Nottingham Victoria during May 1962. Photograph courtesy Rail-Online.

Opposite above WEST HALLAM

Gresley K2 Class 2-6-0 no. 61773 has a local train for Derby in September 1960. The engine was a recent addition to the ranks at Colwick, which has been painted on the bufferbeam, though this only lasted until December when withdrawn. Photograph courtesy Rail-Online.

Opposite below WEST HALLAM STATION

Gresley developed his earlier H2 and H3 (LNER K1 and K2) Class 2-6-0 design to meet evolving freight demands at the end of the First World War, with the H4 (LNER K3) Class 2-6-0. This design had a larger boiler, possessing more superheater elements (32 instead of 24), and three cylinders to provide greater power. Ten appeared. Ten appeared before Grouping, then the design was chosen to be a standard engine for use across the LNER, allowing construction numbers to reach 183 between 1923 and 1937. No. 61896 was the product of Darlington Works in August 1930 as one of nine ordered there and these featured slight detail differences, such as cab design, regulator operation and the grate mechanism. The locomotive is passing through West Hallam station with a freight train for Burton-on-Trent during the 1950s. Colwick-allocated from June 1954 to May 1962 when condemned, no. 61896 has the depot's '38A' code here. Photograph courtesy Rail-Online.

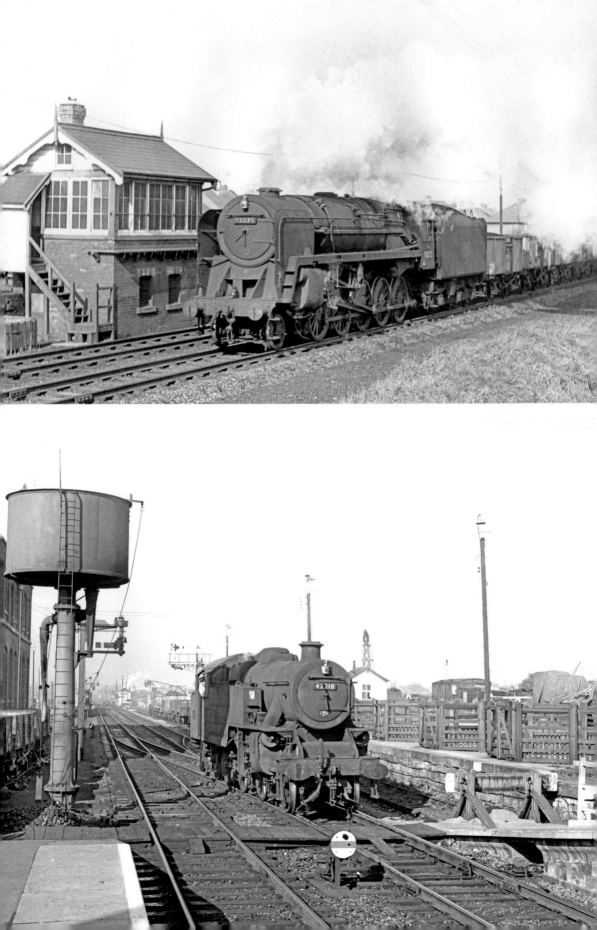

Above WORKSOP

Robinson O4/7 Class 2-8-0 no. 63661 is at Worksop on 8th June 1965 with a ballast train. The engine was built for the ROD by Kitson & Co. in July 1918 and was later part of the second LNER purchase of surplus locomotives which numbered 48. Gorton Works overhauled the locomotive at this time before entering service to Colwick. No. 63661 was later rebuilt under Gresley, with a diagram 15D boiler being fitted, resulting in a reclassification from O4/3 to O4/7; the change occurred in August 1940. Allocated to Retford when pictured, the engine soon moved to Frodingham and was condemned there in August. Photograph by Geoff Warnes.

Opposite above WILFORD

Just south of Nottingham at Wilford on the ex-GCR main line, BR Standard Class 9F no. 92075 has a southbound loaded coal train during the 1960s. Apart from six months at Toton in 1963, the locomotive was Annesley allocated from March 1957 to July 1965. As a result, no. 92075 was one of a number of 9Fs at the depot to be fitted with Briquette Tube Feeders in the tender. This aimed to stop the very hard water used at Annesley from forming scale in the boiler and causing corrosion which increased maintenance. No. 92075 was paired with BR1F tender no. 1164 when new in March 1956 and this type was paired new to all Eastern Region 9Fs. The BR1F design had a higher water capacity than the others paired with the 9Fs at 5,625 gallons and the coal capacity was 7 tons. No. 92075 moved on to Kirkby-in-Ashfield, then Carlisle Kingmoor. The engine was condemned there in September 1966. Photograph courtesy Rail-Online.

Opposite below WORKSOP STATION

View west at Worksop station on 10th October 1964, featuring Fairburn 4P Class 2-6-4T no. 42218. The station was opened by the Manchester, Sheffield & Lincolnshire Railway (later Great Central Railway), in July 1849. Costing nearly £8,000, a Sheffield-based architect used the Jacobean style with locally-sourced Steetley stone for the station building, though the goods station – on the extreme left – was regular red brick. To the west of the station, the GCR built a small gravity concentration yard in the early 20th century to improve capacity on the line. No. 42218 had been London-based from entering traffic in 1946 and recently transferred from Willesden to Kirkby-in-Ashfield in May 1963. The locomotive was shortly to be withdrawn, being marked for scrap at the end of the month. Photograph by Geoff Warnes.

BIBLIOGRAPHY

Allen, C.J. *Titled Trains of Great Britain*. 1983.

Bendall, Ian R. *Industrial Locomotives of Nottinghamshire*. 1999.

Dow, George. *Great Central Volumes One to Three*.

Etherington, A.R. and I.R. Bendall. *Industrial Railways and Locomotives of Leicestershire & South Derbyshire*. 2006.

Griffiths, Roger and John Hooper. *Great Northern Railway Engine Sheds Volume One: Southern Area*. 2001.

Griffiths, Roger and John Hooper. *Great Northern Railway Engine Sheds: Volume Two The Lincolnshire Loop, Nottingham & Derbyshire*. 1996.

Griffiths, Roger and John Hooper. *Great Northern Railway Engine Sheds Volume Three: Lancashire and Yorkshire*. 2000.

Griffiths, Roger and Paul Smith. *The Directory of British Engine Sheds and Principal Locomotive Servicing Points: 2 North Midlands, Northern England and Scotland*. 2000.

Haresnape, Brian. *Fowler Locomotives*. 1997.

Haresnape, Brian. *Stanier Locomotives*. 1974.

Hawkins, Chris and George Reeve. *LMS Engine Sheds: Volume Two The Midland Railway*. 1981.

Hooper, J. *The WD Austerity 2-8-0 – The BR Record*. 2010.

Hunt, David, John Jennison, Fred James and Bob Essery. *LMS Locomotive Profiles: No. 5 – The Mixed Traffic Class 5s Nos 5000-5224*. 2003.

Hunt, David, John Jennison, Fred James and Bob Essery. *LMS Locomotive Profiles: No. 6 – The Mixed Traffic Class 5s Nos 5225-5499 and 4658-4999*. 2004.

Hunt, David, John Jennison, Fred James and Bob Essery. *LMS Locomotive Profiles: No. 7 – The Mixed Traffic Class 5s Caprotti Valve Gear Engines and Class Summary*. 2006.

Hunt, David, John Jennison, Fred James and Bob Essery. *LMS Locomotive Profiles: No. 8 – The Class 8F 2-8-0s*. 2005.

Hunt, David, John Jennison, Bob Essery and Fred James. *LMS Locomotive Profiles: No. 10 – The Standard Class 4 Goods 0-6-0s*. 2007.

Pike, S.N. *Mile by Mile on the LNER*. 1951.

Quick, Michael. *Railway Passenger Stations in Great Britain: A Chronology*. 2009.

RCTS. *A Detailed History of British Railways Standard Steam Locomotives: Volume One Background to Standardisation and the Pacific Classes*. 2007.

RCTS. *A Detailed History of British Railways Standard Steam Locomotives Volume Two: The 4-6-0 and 2-6-0 Classes*. 2003.

RCTS. *A Detailed History of British Railways Standard Steam Locomotives: Volume Four The 9F 2-10-0 Class*. 2008.

RCTS. *Locomotives of the LNER Part 2A: Tender Engines – Classes A1 to A10*. 1978.

RCTS. *Locomotives of the LNER Part 2B: Tender Engines – Classes B1 to B19*. 1975.

RCTS. *Locomotives of the LNER Part 3B: Tender Engines – Classes D1 to D12*. 1980.

RCTS. *Locomotives of the LNER Part 3C: Tender Engines – Classes D13 to D24*. 1981.

RCTS. *Locomotives of the LNER Part 5: Tender Engines – Classes J1 to J37*. 1984.

RCTS. *Locomotives of the LNER Part 6A: Tender Engines – Classes J38 to K5*. 1980.

RCTS. *Locomotives of the LNER Part 6B: Tender Engines – Classes O1 to P2*. 1980.

Sixsmith, Ian. *The Book of the Ivatt Class 4 2-6-0s*. 2012.

Steam for Scrap: The Complete Story. 1993.

Summerson, Stephen. *Midland Railway Locomotives Volume Four: Johnson Classes Part II (Goods and Later Passenger Tender Engines), Deeley, Fowler and LTSR Classes*. 2005.

Tonks, Eric. *The Ironstone Quarries of the Midlands History, Operation and Railways Part Six: The Corby Area*. 1992.

Townsin, Ray. *The Jubilee 4-6-0s*. 2006.

Walmsley, Tony. *Shed by Shed: Part One London Midland*. 2010.

Walmsley, Tony. *Shed by Shed Part Two: Eastern*. 2010.

Waywell, Robin. *Industrial Locomotives of Buckinghamshire, Bedfordshire & Northamptonshire*. 2001.

Wrottesley, John. *The Great Northern Railway Volumes One to Three*.

Also available from Great Northern

The Last Years of Yorkshire Steam

The Golden Age of Yorkshire Railways

Gresley's A3s

Peppercorn's Pacifics

London Midland Steam 1948-1966

The Last Years of North East Steam

British Railways Standard Pacifics

Western Steam 1948-1966

The Last Years of North West Steam

Gresley's V2s

Southern Steam 1948-1967

Yorkshire Steam 1948-1967

Gresley's A4s

Gresley's B17s

The Last Years of West Midlands Steam

visit www.*greatnorthernbooks.co.uk* for details.